To Susanne

With warmest personal regards
and sincere best wishes

Brian Gorman

ATTITUDE THERAPY
FOR
STRESS DISORDERS

Dr. Brian J. Gorman
Calgary, Alberta

Detselig Enterprises Ltd.
Calgary, Alberta

Foreword by Dr. Hans Selye

1979 by Detselig Enterprises Ltd.
6147 Dalmarnock Cr. N.W.
Calgary, Alberta T3A 1H3

Printed in Canada

ISBN 0-920490-03-4

FOREWORD

This is a truly helpful book and I can think of few people better qualified to have written it than Dr. Gorman. All I can add in this foreword is a summary of my own research to underline the compatibility of his approach with the work of a physician.

To see how one's attitude may be linked to stress and physical illness, we must first understand what stress is and what causes it. The word "stress", like "success", "failure", or "happiness", means different things to different people, so that defining it is extremely difficult even though it has become part of our daily vocabulary. Is stress merely a synonym for distress? Is it effort, fatigue, pain, fear, the need for concentration, the humiliation of censure, the frustration of not being able to express one's feelings, or an unexpected great success which requires complete reformulation of one's entire life? The answer is yes and no. That is what makes the definition of stress so difficult. Every one of these conditions produces stress, but none of them can be singled out as being "it", since the word applies equally to all the others.

But how can we cope with the stress of life if we cannot even define it? The businessman who is under constant pressure from his clients and employees alike, the air-traffic controller who knows that a moment of distraction may mean death to hundreds of people, the husband and wife who are unhappily married, the person who is weighed down by guilt and self-doubt, all suffer from stress. The problems they face are totally different, but medical research has shown that in many respects the body responds in a stereotyped manner, with identical biochemical changes, essentially meant to cope with any type of increased demand upon the human machinery. The stress-producing factors — technically called stressors — are different, yet they all elicit essentially the same biological stress response. This distinction between stressor and stress was perhaps the first important step in the scientific analysis of the most common biological phenomenon that we all know only too well from personal experience.

Stress is defined as the nonspecific response of the body to any demand made upon it. To understand this definition we must first explain what we mean by nonspecific. Each demand made upon our body is in a sense unique, that is, specific. When exposed to cold, we shiver to produce more heat, and the blood vessels in our skin contract to diminish the loss of heat from the body surfaces. When exposed to heat, we sweat because the evaporation of perspiration from the surface of our skin has a cooling effect. When we eat too much sugar and the blood-sugar level rises above normal, we excrete some of it and burn up the rest so that the blood sugar returns to normal. Great muscular effort, such as running up many flights of stairs at full speed, makes increased demands upon our musculature and cardiovascular system. The muscles will need supplemental energy to perform this unusual work; hence, the heart will beat more rapidly and strongly, and the blood pressure will rise to dilate the vessels, thereby increasing the flow of blood to the muscles. All drugs or hormones have specific actions.

For example, diuretic drugs increase the production of urine; the hormone adrenaline augments the pulse rate and blood pressure, simultaneously raising blood sugar, whereas the hormone insulin decreases blood sugar.

Yet, no matter what kind of derangement is produced, all these agents have one thing in common; they also increase the demand for adjustment. This demand is nonspecific; it requires adaptation to a problem, irrespective of what that problem may be.

That is, in addition to their specific actions, all agents to which we are exposed also produce a nonspecific increase in the need to perform adaptive functions and thereby to re-establish normalcy. This is independent of the specific activity that caused the rise in requirements. The nonspecific demand for activity as such is the essence of stress.

From the point of view of its stress-producing or stressor activity, it is immaterial whether the agent or situation we face is pleasant or unpleasant; all that counts is the intensity of the demand for readjustment or adaptation. The woman who is suddenly told that her husband died in battle suffers a terrible mental shock; if years later it turns out that the news was false and the husband unexpectedly walks into her room alive and well, she experiences extreme joy. The specific results of the two events, sorrow and joy, are completely different, in fact, opposite to each other, yet their stressor effect — the nonspecific demand to readjust herself to an entirely new situation — may be the same.

Although it is difficult to see how such essentially different things as cold, heat, drugs, hormones, sorrow, and joy could provoke an identical biochemical reaction in the body, this is the case. It can now be demonstrated that certain reactions are totally nonspecific and common to all types of exposure.

It has taken medicine a long time to accept the existence of such a stereotyped response. It did not seem logical that different tasks, in fact any task, should require the same response. Yet, if you come to think of it, there are many analogies in everyday life in which highly specific things or events share the same nonspecific feature.

For example, consider the appliances in a house that has heaters, refrigerators, bells, and light bulbs, which respectively produce heat, cold, sound, or light, in a most specific manner; yet to function they all depend upon one common factor — electricity. A member of a primitive tribe who never heard of electricity would find it very difficult to accept that all the manifold phenomena just mentioned depend upon the satisfaction of common demand: the provision of electrical energy.

Diseases in whose development the nonspecific stressor effects of the eliciting pathogen play a major role are called diseases of adaptation or stress diseases. But just as there is no pure stressor (that is, an agent that causes only the nonspecific response and has no specific action), so there are no pure diseases of adaptation. Some nonspecific components participate in the pathogenesis of every malady, but no disease is due to stress alone. The justification for placing a malady in this category is directly proportional to the role that maladjustment to stress plays in its development. In some instances (for example, surgical shock), stress may be far the most important pathogenic factor. However, in other cases (instantly lethal intoxications, traumatic injuries to the spinal cord, most congenital malformations) it plays little or no role, either because the damage is inflicted so rapidly that there is no time for any adaptive process, or because the pathogen is highly specific. In the latter event, whatever develops represents a secondary result and is not the primary component. Typical diseases of adaptation are due to insufficient, excessive or faulty reactions to stressors, as in inappropriate hormonal or nervous responses.

Some of the diseases in which stress usually plays a particularly important role are high blood pressure, heart accidents, gastric or duodenal ulcers (the "stress ulcers") and various types of mental disturbances. Yet, there is no disease that can be attributed exclusively to maladaptation, since the cause of nonspecific responses will always be modified by various "conditioning factors" that enhance, diminish, or otherwise alter disease-proneness. Most important among these are the body's reactivity by endogenous (hereditary, previously sustained damage to certain organs) or by exogenous (concurrent exposure to other pathogens and environmental agents, diet) conditioners. Hence, the diseases of adaptation cannot be ascribed to any one pathogen but only to "pathogenic constellations"; they belong to what we have called the pluricausal diseases ("multifactorial maladies"), which depend upon the simultaneous effect of several potentially pathogenic factors that alone would sometimes not produce disease.

Important advances have been made in the chemical treatment of stress and stress-linked diseases, ie., the discovery of endorphins which have morphine-like, pain-killing properties and tranquilizers and other psychotherapeutic chemicals. Potent anti-ulcer drugs are also worth mentioning, as they block the pathways through which stress ulcers are produced.

Inevitably we will profit from the enormous progress made in the recognition and treatment of identifiable diseases of the body by modern medicine and surgery, but this is not enough. Now, the greatest challenge faced by the healing professions is to teach people how to live in a way that satisfies them without hurting others. I believe we can achieve this most effectively through the development of a code of behavior that assists us in coping with the stress of life in our increasingly "civilized" world.

All the purely medical discoveries are applicable only by physicians, and the general public cannot use them in daily life without constant medical supervivon. Furthermore, most of these agents are not actually directed against stress but rather against some of its morbid manifestations (ulcers, high blood pressure, heart accidents). Therefore, increasing attention has been given to the development of psychological techniques and behavioral codes that anybody can use after suitable instruction to adjust to the particular demands made by his life.

In this book on attitude therapy for stress-induced disorders, Brian Gorman has reviewed many of the most widely used techniques and therapies. He has gone even further by offering us his own direct and practical approach, i.e., in terms of time, energy, money, etc., for the treatment of the whole person by a selection and combination of the available therapies. He gives us a unified concept encompassing Transactional Analysis, Gestalt Therapy, Reality Therapy, hypnosis and relaxation, and the thoughts of such theorists as Carl Rogers, Stanley Coopersmith and myself.

What it boils down to is this: it doesn't matter what name you give your therapy, but whether it works to help people live fuller, happier lives. Dr. Gorman's approach seems to be doing just that.

As an addition to his excellent book, I would just like to outline the main points of my code of behavior, developed over four decades of clinical and laboratory research.

1. <u>Find your own stress level</u> — the speed at which you can run toward your own goal. Make sure that both the stress level and the goal are really your own, and not imposed upon you by society, for only you yourself can know what you want and how fast you can accomplish it. There is no point in forcing a turtle to run like a racehorse or preventing a racehorse from running faster than a turtle because of some "moral obligation". The same is true of people.

2. <u>Be an altruistic egoist.</u> Do not try to suppress the natural instinct of all living beings to look after themselves first. Yet the wish to be of some use, to do some good to others, is also natural. We are social beings, and everybody wants somehow to earn respect and gratitude. You must be useful to others. This gives you the greatest degree of safety, because no one wishes to destroy a person who is useful.

3. <u>Earn thy neighbour's love,</u> is a contemporary modification of the maxim "Love thy neighbour as thyself." It recognizes that all neighbours are not lovable and that it is impossible to love on command.

Perhaps two short lines can summarize what I have discovered from all my thought and research:

Fight for <u>your</u> highest <u>attainable</u> aim,
but do not put up resistance in vain.

Dr. Hans Selye, President
International Institute of Stress
University of Montreal

CONTENTS

ACKNOWLEDGMENTS

I would like to thank my wife, Joan, and my children, Peter, Alice, and David, for their encouragement, understanding and forebearance, during the preparation of this book, when I gave them very little attention.

Also, I owe a debt to the nurses of the Bashaw General Hospital, especially Pat Hornett and Joy Williams, for their patience and understanding when I belabored them with my theories and diagrams on placemats and table napkins during coffee breaks.

To Dr. Ismail Abrahams, a scholar and clinician of the highest order, who encouraged me when it was most needed, my sincere thanks. My gratitude is also extended to those who kindly read my rough manuscript and offered their constructive and helpful criticism: Dr. Hans Selye (Montreal), who also provided the biological and some of the philosophical source material; to Dr. J. W. McIntyre, Professor of Anaesthesia (Edmonton), whose honest criticism I much appreciated and which sent me back to my study to re-write much of the book; to Dr. Don McNeil (Calgary) and Dr. Martyn Gay (Bristol), who steered me into a more professional approach; to Dr. G. Naylor and Dr. M. D. Brown (Calgary), colleagues who have supported me in my efforts, and to my sisters, Mary Langley and Norah Gorman, for their helpful criticisms and encouragement.

I owe much to Carl Rogers, whose humanistic approach began to let me see that a synthesis could be made of the biological and psychological viewpoints. Much is also owed to Tom Harris, Stanley Coopersmith, Sidney Jourard and the late Eric Berne and Fritz Perls without whose brilliant work I would have had no material with which to formulate a unified concept of therapy.

For the comprehensive statistical analysis of my results (which appears in Appendix D), I am indebted to Dr. Mildslav Nosal, (University of Calgary), Director of the Statistical

Research Laboratory and Mr. William Wakaryk.

My special gratitude and regard is extended to Mrs. Cherry Grier and Mrs. Carney Raitz Wakaryk who devoted many hours to editing the spelling, grammar, style and even propriety of this book. They did much to bring it into a readable form and I hope I am not going to incur their wrath by not taking their sound advice in places where they may have considered the flavor too salty or even distasteful.

I would like also to thank my critics and detractors without whose constant jibes of "unscientific" and "mumbo-jumbo" this book would never have come into existence. Their criticism has been a wonderful stimulus for the long and tedious work of its preparation.

Last, but not least, I would like to thank my secretaries Shirley Horel and Marilyn Cameron for their hours of typing, correction of my spelling and grammatical mistakes and their patience in re-typing those sections in which I kept changing my mind.

INTRODUCTION

First of all, I wish to describe a little about myself and why I am writing this book. Having served for five years in the British Army in World War II and after, and doing a total of 29 different types of work before entering medical school, I tend to be non-conformist in my views about most things.

I qualified at Bristol, England, in 1960, and after doing my internship I came to Canada where I thought I could cure all human ills with my scalpel and prescription pad. I was, therefore, sadly disillusioned when I found that probably seventy percent of the patients coming to see me in my country general practice were suffering from psychosomatic disorders and could not be cured by either.

To my amazement and consternation, I found that I was very poorly trained to deal with the vast majority of the complaints which were presented to me. Patients came in with a variety of symptoms. I would take a comprehensive history, give them a thorough examination and order such laboratory investigations as I thought indicated. What surprised me was the lack of many or all of the physical signs of illness; and the laboratory investigations seemed to produce very little in the way of positive abnormalities, but quite often "deviations from the normal" which were of little or no significance.

At last it began to dawn on me that, in the majority of cases, I was not faced by organic or "real" illness, but rather with the results of STRESS produced by mal-adjustment, unhappiness, failure to grow intellectually, frustration, boredom and snarled-up inter-personal relationships.

In desperation I started prescribing tranquillizers and anti-depressants, but I found very quickly this did not help the patient or do my own self-esteem much good. All it seemed to do was to keep them away from the clinic for a month or so and make the pharmaceutical companies happy; but in no way did it solve their problems.

I began to realize that, with the exception of the antibiotics, pesticides and fungicides, and the vaccines in preventive medicine, most of our medications were purely palliative in nature — they helped you to live with your disease. I started to think that those of my patients who suffered from physical disorders triggered by emotional stress should perhaps be seeing psychiatrists. When I did persuade one or two patients with ulcers or migraine to see a psychiatrist, they were promptly asked if they had hallucinations or delusions and when they said, "No, I have an ulcer", they were told they had come to the wrong department!

I realized the psychiatrists were not trained or orientated towards dealing with psychosomatic disease. An enormous gulf existed between the General Practitioner, Internist, Gastro-Enterologist, Neurologist and Psychiatrist into which were herded all those patients with stress disorders. They were instructed to take their tranquilizers, anti-depressants, pain killers, etc., three times a day for the next thirty-five years or so and they would be alright.

I then purchased and read the latest psychiatric textbooks and found these dealt, almost exclusively, in an arbitrary (and to my mind, unnatural) sorting and classifying of the various categories of "mental illness" and made very little reference to methods of treating them.

Hoping to find some more positive approach to therapy, I began to turn to the "Positive Thinkers". I read *Psycho-Cybernetics* by Maxwell Maltz (17), *The power of Positive Thinking* by Norman Vincent Peal (18), and many others. They all agreed that one only had to give oneself "positive thoughts" in order to be completely transformed. I found them to be inspiring but impractical. Besides, their theories clashed with Emil Coue's (4) Law of Inverse Effort, which says, "The harder you try, the less likely you are to succeed".

This led me to broaden my reading and I turned to the Behaviorists: Watson (29), Skinner (24), Salter (22), Lazarus (14), for example. Here I found that the human being was considered to be a mass of reflexes which had been conditioned by external forces (mainly repressive) to act in a manner which was mainly repressed (or inhibited). Behavior Therapy consisted mainly in a number of exercises designed to overcome these repressions. This seemed to me to be only partly true.

I then came upon the works of William Glasser (7) in *Reality Therapy* and other books. These seemed to be dealing with patients who were certainly not repressed but actually rebellious. The works of Abraham Maslow (16) were then added, with his concept of the innate drive of every person to grow psychologically, to fulfill his full potential, to become "Self-Actualized".

I did not, of course, exclude Freud (6) from my readings. I came to the conclusion that he was the most careful and penetrating clinical observer, and that many of his observations and descriptions still stand today. His theories of the Conscious, Pre-Conscious and Unconscious and the scientific approach which he used undoubtedly made him the founder of modern psychiatry. However, his interpretations of some of the conditions which he so beautifully described seemed to leave much to be desired. It seemed every interpretation was a sick one and no psychologically "healthy" person existed.

My next adventure was into hypnosis and I found this a fascinating study and a useful tool in dealing with a limited number of conditions. However, I found that good results were not sustained and patients tended to relapse unless the therapy was bolstered by changes in attitude and behavior. Hypnosis seemed to be good for "switching off" stress reactions. But if faulty attitudes and behavior allow the stress to be "turned on" again, then the hypnosis seems to have less and less effect.

Gestalt Therapy became the next school to investigate. Here I found that it did not matter what you understood or how you behaved as long as you *felt* right. This struck me as somewhat impractical because any rational thought was banned as some sort of sin. However, their concepts of "Awareness" and "Living in the Now" certainly seemed to have some merit.

My reading was beginning to produce a formidable number of seemingly conflicting and unrelated theories and therapies, with each "school" dogmatically devoted to proving it was right. Parallel to these readings, I was following the works of Hans Selye

(23) of Montreal, in his lifelong research into the biological aspects of stress.

It was not until I began to study the "Interactional Psychologists" such as Carl Rogers (21) in *On Becoming a Person*, Eric Berne (1) in *Transactional Analysis in Psychotherapy*, and Sidney Jourard (13) in *The Transparent Self* that I began to see that perhaps all these various schools could be put together into a unified concept of psychotherapy which would not only deal with thought, emotional and behavior disorders, but also those physical disorders triggered by stress.

I slowly began to evolve a method of treatment which integrated the biological and psychological aspects of stress and formulated a concept which consisted, first of all, in an explanation, to the patient of the mechanisms of stress, and its relationship to disease, based upon the monumental work of Hans Selye. I would explain how we had to attack the Alarm Phase of his General Adaptation Syndrome and that it had to be with a combination of four components:

1. **Attitude Modification.** This consisted in a theory of personality, using, as a skelton, the theories of Transactional Analysis; with flesh and muscle being added with the theories of Carl Rogers, Stanley Coopersmith (3), Fritz Perls (20), Tom Harris (10) and Hans Selye.

2. **Behavior Modification.** I had to agree with the Behaviorists that indeed much of our illness, both mental and physical, is due to repression, inhibition, manipulation; allowing ourselves to be walked upon, used, abused and mistreated. Therefore, behavior modification in the form of Assertiveness Training is necessary to prevent the anxieties, depressions, ulcers, asthma, hypertension, migraine, tension headaches and a whole host of stress-related diseases.

3. **Relaxation.** Few of us can relax sufficiently well to "switch off" the stresses of life before they have triggered the alarm reactions in our body, so I use Self-Hypnosis as an important part of my method, but I stress that, by itself, it is not enough unless accompanied by Attitude and Behavior Modification.

If a particular person or situation can trigger a migraine, I may use hypnosis to take it away. However, if I continually return to the same circumstances which precipitated the attack and, each time, I go into my quiet room and use hypnosis before returning to the stressful environment, then the hypnosis will have less and less effect. Therefore, while learning to deal with the migraine by hypnosis, I must also alter my attitude and behavior under those circumstances so that no person or situation can precipitate a migraine. The results of hypnosis will then be permanent and I shall have less and less recourse to its use.

The same can also be said of Transcendental Meditation (a form of Self-Hypnosis with cultural overtones), Yoga (a form of Self-Hypnosis with religious and cultural overtones) and Biofeedback (a method of feeding back to oneself his own biological functions until he learns to control them). All of these modalities of treatment must be backed up by attitude and behavior modification if the results are to be sustained.

4. **The Character of the Relationship.** It seemed to be necessary that any theory had to be applied within the framework of a relationship between therapist and patient which satisfied certain clearly defined characteristics.

I did not intend to write a book; I set out to treat patients, but then I found I was having to do a lot of explanation which was repetitive. About four years ago, a patient was sent to me by a druggist because she had migraine and was consuming large quantities of pain killers. When I first met her, it was obvious she did not want to tell me much about herself. I, therefore, obtained only a meagre history before starting to explain my theories. She listened in silence for an hour and departed. The next week, she returned, and I continued doing most of the talking. This went on for six consecutive weeks and at the end of the sixth session she said, "Thank you very much, doctor. You have helped me enormously. I have not had a headache for three weeks and have stopped taking pain killers. I don't think I need to see you again." She shook me by the hand and left.

I thought: "Hey, I don't even know what your underlying problem is yet!", and then I wondered if she was just trying to tell me, politely, that I could not help her.

I was, therefore, greatly surprised when she sent about a dozen patients to me during the next six months, all of whom said that I had helped her very much. I began to realize that she had been able to listen to my theories and fit herself into the framework in such a way as to solve her own problems without even letting me know what they were! It occurred to me that perhaps other people could do the same and the need for time spent in individual therapy could be much reduced. Hence this book.

1
Stress
and
Disease

This chapter is intended to give the reader a theoretical basis for the psychological treatment of those physical and emotional disorders triggered by stress. I am going to lean rather heavily on the works of Dr. Hans Selye, of Montreal, in his tremendous research work in this field so I would like first to give an outline of some of his basic concepts.

Hans Selye describes life as a series of adaptations to the world in which we live. Health is the successful adjustment to the changing surroundings of our environment. Disease is a failure to keep the process of adaptation within the homeostatic limits as suggested by Walter Cannon, the pioneer physiologist.

As a young student, Dr. Selye was struck by the similarity of many patients who were, as yet, undiagnosed, but who presented with what he called "the syndrome of being sick". They looked and felt sick and had fever, malaise, disordered bowel action, loss of appetite and perhaps abdominal pain. Some had diffuse aches and pains of the joints.

Later, as a research worker, he was endeavoring to find a new hormone in the ovary and he found that if ground-up extracts of ovary were injected into rats and ten days later they were killed, at autopsy, they all showed three distinct features:

a. Ulceration of the stomach and small intestines,
b. Enlargement of the adrenal glands (the hormone glands responsible for the bodily defence against stress),
c. Degeneration of the thymus gland (behind the breast-bone) and

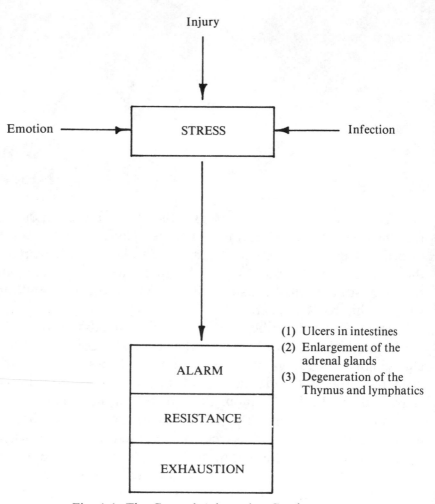

Fig. 1-1. The General Adaptation Syndrome

the lymphatic system, which, between them produce the body's defences against infection and allergy.

He then found to his disgust these same features could also be caused by injection of extracts of pituitary, placenta, kidney, spleen and other organs. He began to realize these three features may just be the result of applying stress to the animal by injuring it with injections of foreign material. He then injected rats with a dilute solution of formalin and produced the same features. He realized this was not the result of any new hormone, but the nonspecific effects of tissue drainage, which he called **The General Adaptation Syndrome**. Subsequent experiments showed that infections, injury or emotional stress caused the same results.

The General Adaptation Syndrome was divided into three distinct phases. If rats were subjected to stress and killed shortly afterwards they showed all the acute manifestations and he called this **The Alarm Phase**.

He then subjected rats to stress and left them for longer periods and killed them. He found that all those acute manifestations had subsided and that the animal had apparently learned to cope with its stress. This he called **The Resistance Phase**.

When he subjected rats to stress and left them for much longer periods, he found they would ultimately die and at autopsy would show that the three original features characteristic of stress had recurred in sufficiently massive form to kill the animal. This he called **The Phase of Exhaustion**. Thus, he found the animals had a limited capacity to deal with stress and when the adaptive reserves were used up the animal died.

He then began working on the pathways through which stress operated and Dr. Selye's main research was on the hormone pathway. Starting with the Pituitary Gland (the master hormone gland under the brain); and working through the adrenal glands and, to a lesser extent, the other hormone glands, he was able to show how a whole host of diseases could be caused.

Hormone-Induced Diseases

The Pituitary gland produces a number of hormones in response to stress, the main ones being ACTH (Adreno-Cortico-Trophic Hormone), which stimulates the adrenal glands and suppresses inflammation and STH (Somato-Trophic Hormone) which stimulates growth and promotes inflammation. The Adrenal glands produce cortisone and adrenaline which act upon the kidneys, which, in their turn, produce Renal Pressor Substances which cause hypertension leading to kidney and heart disease. Adrenaline and cortisone both mobilize sugar from the fat depots and thus cause diabetics to become unstable.

Cortisone suppresses the lymphatic tissues which are responsible (a) for defence against infection and (b) for immunity and allergic hyper-sensitivity reactions. Thus we get allergy, asthma and eczema. Cortisone also produces ulceration of the stomach and duodenum; but the cause of ulceration of the terminal small intestine (Crohn's disease) and ulcerative colitis is still obscure, although they are possibly stress related.

The Brain and Spinal Cord

Besides the hormone path of stress, it is a fact which has long been established in clinical practice that the brain and spinal cord constitute a major path through which stress shows itself. Stress affecting the brain causes emotional disorders (anxiety, depression), thought disorders (hallucinations, delusions, paranoid feelings), and behavior disorders (alcoholism, obesity, etc.). To anyone who doubts whether stress can produce hallucinations, I would suggest standing in a foxhole, at night, trying to keep your eyes on a row of bushes. After about an hour you would swear that they were, in actual fact, enemy soldiers creeping towards you.

One patient developed a tingling of his left hand when his Department was being criticized and this stopped when the criticism stopped.

One executive developed pain in his feet (even while driving his car) when he was under nervous stress. Reduction of tension caused the pain to be alleviated.

Stress affecting the spinal cord causes the muscles supplied by the spinal nerves to go into spasm thus creating tension headaches, low back pain, or muscle pain, spasm or twitching anywhere.

The Autonomic Nervous System

If emotion can control the size of blood vessels, then emotion could cause migraine, impotence or Raynaud's phenomenon. It has been recognized for many years that if you are frightened you turn pale; if embarrassed you flush; if you are angered you may have a heart attack or stroke. This indicates clearly that there is direct autonomic nervous system control of blood vessels.

The spasm of the smooth muscles of the bronchial tubes in asthma has long been considered to be an expression of repressed anger; and we have all been aware of the knot in the stomach brought on by fear or tension. Therefore, "nervous stomach", "nervous colitis", and menstrual pains could also be considered psychosomatic disorders. The lungs are the third target of disorder of the autonomic nervous system and we may get hysterical over-breathing leading to tetany, numbness, tingling and fainting.

I would, therefore, like to put together the pathways of stress into a comprehensive diagram showing the three main components:

1. Hormonal
2. Cerebro-spinal
3. Autonomic

As we can see from the enlarged diagram of stress, a whole host of recognizable symptom complexes and diseases can be produced by stress of one nature or another. What do we tend to do about this?

1. *With thyrotoxicosis* we suppress thyroid function or do a partial thyroidectomy.

2. *With peptic ulcers* we give bedrest, sedation, bland diets, antacids and anti-spasmodics or histamine blockers.

3. *With unstable diabetes* we balance the insulin, diet and exercise.

4. *With infections* we treat with antibiotics.

5. *With allergy* we give desensitizing injections.

6. *With asthma* we give broncho-dilators, mucolitic agents and perhaps steroids.

7. *With eczema* we give cortisone or its derivatives in cream form.

8. *With hypertension* we give medication to lower the blood pressure.

9. *With congestive heart failure* we give digitalis, diuretics and reduced salt diets.

10. *With rheumatoid arthritis* we give anti-inflammatory corticoids, aspirin and similar medications.

11. *With tension headaches* we give tranquillizers, analgesics and muscle relaxants.

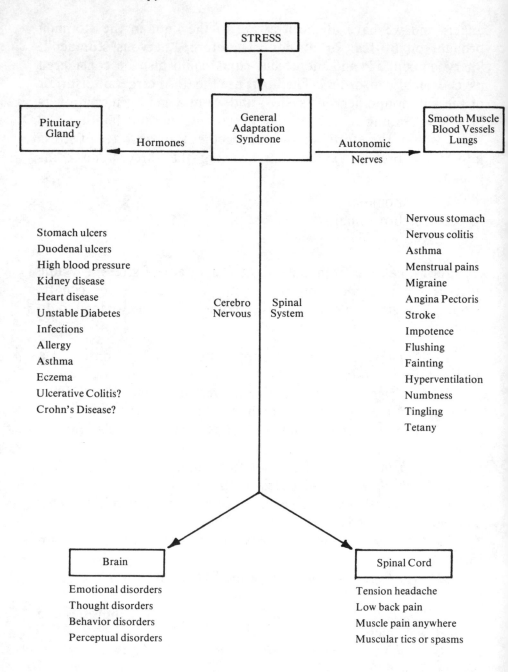

Fig. 1-2. Stress and Disease

12. *With gastro-intestinal colics* we give smooth muscle relaxants and analgesics.

13. *With migraine headaches* we give Ergot preparations, pain killers, tranquilizers and a host of other medications.

14. *With angina pectoris* we give Nitroglycerine and other vasodilators.

15. *With emotional disorders* we give the minor tranquillizers.

16. *With thought disorders* we give the major tranquillizers.

17. *With behavior disorders* we lock them up.

18. *With period pains* we tell them to get pregnant.

19. *With impotence* we reassure them and shrug it off.

What we are doing is treating syndromes symptomatically. Now, I quite agree that if a patient is subjected to injury or massive infection, or if the disease has progressed to the stage of irreversible organic change, psychotherapy is not of much use except as an adjunct which can perhaps arrest the advance of the condition.

However, I am sure you will agree that psychological stress is a major factor which brings patients to our clinics, and if we could attack the General Adaptation Syndrome in the early phase of the Alarm Reaction by psychotherapy, many of these conditions could be prevented, arrested, or aborted.

If this statement is valid, then we should be able to treat, by psychotherapy, such widely diverse conditions as peptic ulcers, colitis, unstable diabetes, allergy, asthma, eczema, hypertension, tension headaches, or muscle pains anywhere, gastro-intestinal colics, menstrual pains, migraine, impotence or angina.

This is precisely what I have been doing for the past eight years. You may say "What psychotherapy?" or "How do you apply it?". There are so many and divergent "schools" and opinions and methods. About fourteen years ago I started to study the various types of psychotherapy and attended numerous courses and workshops in each and found that the analytical schools believed insight into childhood trauma was the magic key. The Behaviorists believed that all would be well if you were conditioned to respond appropriately to certain stimuli; the Gestaltists believed that it did not matter what you understood or how you behaved as long as you felt right; and the third force or transactional schools (Berne, Rogers, Harris, Jourard) felt that the character of the inter-personal relationships was all important. Finally, the "turn-off" schools believed that all these were unnecessary and that all one had to do was to put oneself into hypnosis or to meditate or practice yoga for the conditions to be resolved.

To my psychiatrically untrained mind it seemed they all had tunnel vision and what we needed was a composite method which makes use of those proven portions of each school. The primitive form of reaction to stress was either that of flight or fight. In our much more complex society today there are many forms of stress from which we can neither run away nor stand and fight — the income tax demand, the mortgage payment, the bank overdraft, the unhappy marriage, the loss of loved ones or the break-up of a marriage, whether your own or your parents, will still trigger off the Alarm Reaction of the General Adaptation Syndrome. This reaction, once started, cannot initiate any useful action, which was its primitive purpose; and therefore tends to become internalized and will show itself in a number of ways: I can think of six ways in which people commonly react to stress — four of them unhealthy and two of them healthy.

The diagram is more or less self-explanatory with regard to emotional disorders and the physical or psychosomatic disorders I have already spoken about but I will elaborate a little on some of the others.

Thought Disorders

Thomas Szasz (27) in his book *The Myth of Mental Illness* feels that most, if not all, disorders of thought are a process of "copping out" or retreating into a world of fantasy and becoming "crazy" to escape from the pressures of the world. I cannot agree entirely because there is so much we don't know about brain function and there are certain definite organic brain disorders such as *G.P.I., cerebro-vascular insufficiency, cerebral tumors, etc., which are not precipitated by stress. However, he could be right in

*General Paralysis of the Insane

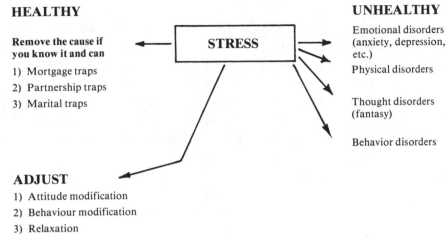

Fig. 1-3. Common Ways of Dealing With Stress

quite a large percentage of such cases. Obviously, when a person has lost contact with reality, psychotherapy is ineffective and drugs have to be used; but even these patients have lucid intervals during which they may be reached.

Behavior Disorders

The pressures of work may become so intense that a person will go home and beat up his wife; a wife may nag her husband incessantly, so he starts to take in the beer parlor or the cocktail lounge on his way home; a husband may go home and completely ignore his wife, who has been sitting at home all day with no communication with other people so she starts to eat or drink to excess. These behavior disorders may result in one or both of them ending up in the magistrate's court, divorce court, Weight Watchers, or Alcoholics Anonymous.

The healthy forms of dealing with stress are either to remove the cause, if you know it, and if you can, or to adjust to the stresses in such a way that they are not allowed to interfere with one's normal functioning.

1. Remove the cause if you know it and can. Harry Browne (2) in a book called *How I found Freedom in an Unfree World*, which I heartily recommend, talks about a large number of traps in which we can ensnare ourselves. I shall mention just a few of them.

a. The identity trap. This is the belief that you should live your life according to standards which other people think you should live up to. In attempting to deal with them I often misquote the "Gestalt Prayer" as follows:
"I do my thing, you do yours,
I will not live my life according to your standards,
Nor will I expect you to live yours according to mine.
If we meet, that's beautiful, if we don't — to hell with it!"

b. The morality trap — Living your life by standards of "right" and "wrong", "good" and "bad", which are imposed upon you by others.

c. The partnership trap. Many people get themselves into partnerships which, at first, seem compatible but which turn out to be a millstone around one's neck. The partner who works slowly, doesn't pull his weight, takes more vacations than anyone and still insists upon an equal share of the profits.

d. The investment trap. So, you buy some stocks and instead of going up they go down! You hold on and hold on, seeing your savings devalue by the minute.

e. The box trap. This is any situation you get yourself into which you feel you cannot get out of. A doctor may decide after fifteen years that he doesn't like medicine, a teacher may decide he doesn't like teaching, an accountant finds he loathes accounting for the earnings of a real estate agent. A box trap could also be considered any trap which has no door. If I lose my leg, I have to learn to live in my box without allowing it to constrict me.

f. The marriage trap. Some people suffer through life in an unsatisfactory marriage "because of the children" or because of the financial losses involved.

Browne goes on to consider many more types of traps but they all have one thing in common. Every trap has a door through which you enter and you can get out through the same door . . . . if you are prepared to accept the price. The price may be in terms of what society will think of you; it may be in the unhappiness of children in a broken marriage; it may be loss of a great deal of money. Whatever the cost one has to decide whether one can afford to pay that cost or whether the price is too high. If you decide that your freedom and happiness is worth $50,000 or $100,000 to get out of a partnership or a marriage, pay it and smile . . . you are free!

It is never too late to change your profession or life style, if this change is going to remove the cause of your stress. If you decide the cost in terms of, say, the happiness of your children, is too great, then you have to adjust . . . you have to learn to change your attitudes in such a way that your trap is no longer constrictive, that you can learn to live happily within your trap. This brings me to the second healthy way of dealing with stress: Adjustment.

2. Adjustment. I have been developing a system based upon:

a. Attitude modification. Faulty attitudes acquired from our parents, society, the church, can cause much internal conflict which triggers the Alarm Reaction and produces the symptoms we have discussed.

b. Behavior modification. This is necessary where abnormal behavior patterns are causing distress. You may be under considerable stress because you are allowing people to manipulate you or "walk all over you". The aim here is to change the primitive reactions of flight or fight to those of non-aggressive assertiveness.

c. Relaxation or self-hypnosis. I like to think of this as a means of "switching off" the Alarm Reaction whenever it is switched on by people or situations. Some therapists use meditation, yoga or biofeedback to achieve the same results. I feel, however, that none of these are as useful as hypnosis and all of them (including hypnosis) suffer the same limitations in that they are unlikely to be permanently effective unless backed by alterations in attitude and behavior.

d. Character of the relationship. I agree heartily with Rogers that unless I can establish a relationship with the patient which includes Self-Acceptance, Congruence, Empathy and Positive Unconditional Regard, then I am unlikely to achieve positive results.

Freud considered that it was necessary to see a patient for three hours a week for two years, or about 300 hours, to achieve results and his results were poor. He did very little talking until he delivered his final analysis. Rogers, in the early fifties, considered that 50 to 80 hours were necessary in his "Client-Centered Therapy" to effect change. His results were considerably better. He did some talking, but restricted himself to paraphrasing the patient, or repeating in his words what the patient had said, in the hope that, within this time, the patient would begin to understand that he was being understood.

I consider that if I have not helped the patients to change their attitudes in ten sessions I am unlikely to do so! My results seem good. I tend to talk a lot because I feel that both Rogers and Freud were underestimating the intelligence of their patients; and that if I can explain precisely what I am trying to do and define my terms and methods, I can cut out 290 hours of Freud's treatment and between 40 and 70 hours of Rogers'.

I do a lot of talking during the first six sessions during which I get a considerable amount of feedback. I allow the patients to tell me where *they* fit into the theoretical framework which I am outlining. *I* do not tell them where they fit because it is a well-known fact that you cannot teach anybody anything. All you can do is to give them the information to enable them to learn for themselves. The average session, with the average feedback, takes one hour. Some people give much more feedback and it may take one and a quarter hours or one and a half hours to cover the same ground. My average is six or seven sessions and virtually never do I exceed ten.

I freely admit that I do not have uniformly successful results with all the conditions listed in the diagram. Some respond well, some poorly, and some not at all.

A statistical evaluation of the results of therapy is included before the Summary and Conclusions, and I feel these results are sufficiently good in the areas of migraine, tension headaches, eczema, asthma, period pains, and freefloating anxiety (or what I call "the tranquilizer-dependent horde") to indicate the treatment is being applied at the Alarm Phase of the General Adaptation Syndrome.

On a practical basis I have classified my results into four categories:

1. Those who become worse during treatment. I have to include this as there is no doubt that some patients have continued to deteriorate despite my best efforts and I have had to refer them elsewhere or resort to traditional medical or surgical treatment.

2. Those who show no apparent change. If I have not achieved results in ten sessions then I generally do not pursue this form of therapy further.

3. Loss of symptoms. This includes those people who may lose their migraine or heal their ulcer or lose their tension headaches or their free-floating anxiety but are still unable to cope successfully with new or varied types of stress.

4. Those who lose their symptoms and change their attitude in such a way that it enables them to deal successfully with different stress situations.

It is sometimes very hard to categorize patients in that perhaps they may have changed and I was not aware of it. For example, about three years ago I saw a lady only three times with migraine and then she disappeared before I thought she was ready to discontinue treatment. I considered her to belong to category no. 2, i.e., no apparent change. I was, therefore, somewhat surprised, when seeing the lady about a year ago with one of her children, who had bronchitis, I asked her, "How are your migraines?". "Oh", she replied, "I haven't had any since I saw you two years ago; and not only that, but I have been able to deal with everything else that has occurred since." This meant that whereas I had placed her in category no. 2, she really belonged in category no. 4, which I consider to be the excellent result group.

I therefore feel the information which I have given in this chapter indicates that stress is the cause of many of our common and debilitating illnesses; that much of the stress is caused by emotional factors; and that we should be thinking much more in terms of psychotherapy for a radical cure rather than the more palliative forms of traditional therapy.

2
A
Theory of
Personality

I think one of the main reasons why there has not been a unified concept of psychotherapy is because there has not been a unified theory of personality. Each school has its own theory and this inevitably seemed to conflict with the theories of the opposing schools. I must admit to being completely baffled by learning that the Freudians believed in a conscious, pre-conscious, and unconscious; whereas the Behaviorists refuted this completely out of hand and stated boldly, upon their observations of rats and other lower forms, that we were just a mass of conditioned reflexes.

It struck me that both could not be entirely correct and yet it did not mean that both were entirely incorrect. Could there not indeed be some valid link between these two seemingly diametrically opposed concepts? Where, also, could we fit those successes achieved by the Gestaltists and the Reality Therapists, the Hypnotists, the Positive Thinkers, the Transcendental Meditators, and those who obtain relief from their symptoms through plain catharsis, either in the confessional or the consulting room?

The theories of Structural and Transactional Analysis, expounded by Eric Berne and further amplified in the excellent book *I'm O.K. — You're O.K.* by Dr. T. A. Harris, allowed me to see that in them lay the skeleton, as it were, of the theory of personality upon which we could add those theories of the other schools which gave flesh and substance to the body of Transactional Analysis. In this way I began to find that their theories were not as diametrically opposed as I had thought. It was possible to reconcile the conscious, pre-conscious and unconscious with the theories of Conditioned Reflex Therapy, Gestalt and Reality Therapy, and indeed, I have been using a combination of all these therapies, depending on the need of the patient, with growing success over a number of years.

I have one main complaint against both the Psycho-Analytical school and the Rogerian Client-Centered method. In the former, too much emphasis is based upon the training, personal qualities and prejudices of the therapist. In the latter method, the patient's statements are all paraphrased or repeated to him in the therapist's words so that the patient will himself derive insight or understanding of his complaint and the remedy. This can, I believe, be shortened considerably, and in some cases the need for individual therapy can be eliminated, by the therapist stating from the start what his theory of personality is and how the patient can see himself and his problems within this framework and take the necessary steps to overcome his problem.

THE SKELETON OF PERSONALITY

Eric Berne, in his pioneer work, observed that when dealing with patients they all seemed to present not one personality but three, which were distinct entities, apparently unrelated (at least on the surface) and between which the patient could jump in the twinkling of an eye. At one moment the patient could be factual, knowledgeable, reasonable and mature just as an adult; but within an instant he could become coy, petulant, boastful, aggressive, mischievous and portray the tone, facial expression and movements of a child. Seconds later he could exhibit all the dogma, prejudice, and inconsistency of a parent. He, therefore, put forward the theory that the human personality was indeed made up of three separate parts, each distinct and each with its own functions. These he called the Parent, Adult, and Child.

Some may complain that he was only putting new names to the three parts of the personality described by Freud, namely the Id, Ego, and Super-Ego. However, the differences between these states is quite marked and must be fully understood before a grasp is obtained of the foundation upon which I am going to try to build the complete theory of personality.

The Id

Freud considered the Id to be the fundamental source of psychic energy. It was disorganized and not in contact with reality. It was the seat of the instincts and drives. Its main function was the fulfillment of the need for pleasure, which he called the primary process. He considered the Id could not be changed by external forces because it was not in contact with these forces. It was not governed by reason and did not possess any sense of values or morality. Its sole purpose was the gratification of its need for pleasure. He considered the Id to be a spoiled child, demanding and irrational; and that it retained these characteristics throughout life. During the process of maturation, however, the Id becomes more and more under the control of the Ego.

The Ego

Freud considered the Ego to be that part of the personality which controls and governs the Id and Super-Ego and retains contact with reality. The Ego is governed by the reality principle, which is to postpone the gratification of one's needs until this can be done reasonably. This was described as the secondary process because it developed after the primary process of the Id.

The Super-Ego

This was considered by Freud to be the moral or ethical branch of the personality. It is made up of two parts: The Ego-Ideal, which is what the child learns from his parents as "good" and the conscience, which is what the child learns from his parents as "bad". The Super-Ego contains the script of life, presented to the individual by his parents, containing all the values and ideals of the particular culture which are handed down from parent to child.

Freud considered the Ego was formed out of the Id and the Super-Ego was formed out of the Ego and that they continue to interact with each other throughout life. This differs in some respects from the concepts of Eric Berne in which the Child and the Parent are operative from birth onwards but the Adult begins to function at about ten months to one year of age. In Structural Analysis, the personality develops in three distinct parts at three different, though overlapping times and with three specific but inter-related functions. The first part to develop is *the Child*.

THE CHILD

This is a complex mass of all the feelings, needs and drives of the growing personality. It is by far the most sensitive part of the personality. It is the creative part, the feeling part, the needing part, the fun part; but it is also the part which hurts and needs to be protected.

The Feelings of the Child Ego State

These include all our fun, curiosity, wonder, delight and pleasure. It is the Child which enjoys the thrill of a game, the anticipation of Christmas, the intimacy of sharing, the feel of the warm sand on the beach, the wonders of sex. It is the Child who lets himself go and says and does things which "respectable" people consider "naughty", "immature" or "childish".

I feel the predominant early feelings of the Child are those of insecurity, anxiety and dependency, as the child is totally incapable of doing anything for himself and must rely on his mother for the security of being held, fed, loved and protected.

Two of the important factors contributing to the early feelings of the Child are the shock of birth and its subsequent complete dependence upon its mother. For several years thereafter, it is, to a lesser and lesser extent dependent upon its parents or their substitutes.

The basic feelings of the Child part of the personality in early life are, therefore "Not O.K." feelings. These tend to change as the person becomes more independent, but we tend to revert to our "Not O.K." feelings from time-to-time throughout life if our needs are not fulfilled.

The second function of the Child ego state is the fulfillment of a great vacuum of *needs*, which must be satisfied if the child is to overcome his "Not O.K." feelings about himself.

The needs of the child are:

1. Stimulation
2. Recognition
3. Structure

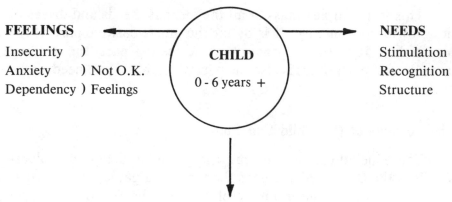

FEELINGS

Insecurity   )
Anxiety   ) Not O.K.
Dependency) Feelings

CHILD

0 - 6 years +

NEEDS

Stimulation
Recognition
Structure

DRIVES

Self-Preservation
Pleasure
Preservation of the species
Fulfillment of potential

Fig. 2-1. The Child

Stimulation

A baby needs to see movement, light, changes in color and surroundings. It needs to have toys hanging from its crib. It needs to be touched, tickled, held, nursed and stroked. It needs to hear voices and footsteps. Without these stimuli a baby will fail to thrive, it will withdraw into itself and it may even die of some minor infection. In World War II in Germany, there were some instances of large orphanages containing many babies with very few nurses to look after them. The nurses only had time to go around every four hours and prop a bottle in the baby's mouth against the pillow, and to change the diapers once each shift. The babies began to die and it was some while before the reason was discovered. The babies were dying of emotional deprivation. The ladies from the district were then encouraged to come in and hold the babies while they were being fed and they stopped dying. This need for stimulation remains with us all our lives and this is why solitary confinement is one of the worst forms of punishment.

Recognition

The second need of the child is that of recognition. This is to help it to begin to develop a sense of identity. Almost every parent has been nearly driven to distraction by the constant demands to "Look Mummy", "Look Daddy", "Watch me stand on my head, Daddy", "Watch me jump off this wall, Mummy". These are all desperate cries of the child for the recognition which he needs for survival as a unique individual, in order to counterbalance the "Not O.K." feelings with which he was born. Every time we fail to give our child the stimulation and recognition which he craves, we are obstructing him from developing the "I'm O.K." feelings which he needs in order to become a mature, well-adjusted adult.

Structure

The third need of the Child is to have his time structured or filled in for him. How many times have you heard your son or daughter say, "What can I do, Daddy"? It is no good telling them to go and play with the toys they received for Christmas or telling them to go and ride their bicycle, because they want you to do it with them, not for the sake of the game itself but for the recognition and stroking which they derive from your undivided attention. This need for recognition and significance in your eyes is the paramount need of the Child, without which he cannot overcome his "Not O.K." feelings, and develop a strong sense of identity. As the person grows older, this need does not diminish to any great extent but the methods of gratifying it change. At the age of fifty, I still have these needs. But if I go out and ask my secretary what to do, she would think I am crazy. Therefore, we have had to develop a whole system of satisfying our needs in a socially-acceptable way.

The methods of structuring our time have been divided into:
1. Rituals
2. Pastimes
3. Activities
4. Games
5. Withdrawal
6. Intimacy

1. **Rituals.** A ritual is a set of transactions between two or more people which is relatively meaningless. It is for the purpose of recognizing their presence and giving them a psychological stroke in a socially acceptable manner.

I may say: "Good Morning, how are you?", to which you may reply: "Very well thanks, how are you?" Neither of us really wants an answer to our question, but we wanted to show more interest than a straight "Good Morning".

If I walk past you in the morning without saying anything, you may think, "What the hell is wrong with him?" (if you feel O.K. about yourself), or, "What have I done wrong?" (if you don't feel O.K. about yourself).

Rituals are superficial means of getting strokes, and we all have certain individuals from whom we expect to get two, ten or twenty strokes, so that the average person may expect to get several hundred in the course of a day.

2. **Pastimes.** Pastimes are sets of exchanges or transactions between two or more people. They are more meaningful than rituals but the topics are superficial and still not important. They are designed to give everyone the maximum recognition. They usually deal with topics which are non-controversial and in which nobody is "put down" or hurt. Pastimes are "small talk". Everybody is included in the conversation and everyone's Child has his needs fulfilled. At a cocktail party, all of the men may gather at one end of the room and discuss cars, hockey, or the stock market. At the other end of the room, the ladies may discuss babies, clothes, art or literature, and as long as everyone has his say and is listened to, everyone will consider it a wonderful party even though they say exactly the same things to the same people as they did at a similar party the week before. If, however, one person does not

know anything about hockey or literature and gets left out of the conversation his Child will feel emotionally deprived and he may well think what a rotten party it is.

3. **Activities.** Activities are useful ways of filling in time, such as work or sports. Very few people can work alone. Perhaps the artist, the sculptor, the painter can work alone for fairly prolonged periods but they are in effect deferring their strokes until the moment they reveal their masterpiece. Most of us need to work with other people in order to get our daily quota of strokes. Most of the satisfaction derived from playing tennis or golf is derived from the fact that you are doing it with someone you like and you are attaining feelings of significance from that person and in turn, making him feel significant in your eyes. Activities are, therefore, performed for three reasons:

 (i) to earn a living:

 (ii) to obtain strokes, and

 (iii) to achieve feelings of competence.

I must feel right about myself.

4. **Games.** Games differ from rituals, pastimes, and activities in that these first three forms of filling in time are basically honest. When I say, "Good morning, Jack", I'm not trying to "con" you, whereas games are all basically dishonest. They have an ulterior motive; and that motive is to derive satisfaction for me at your expense. I may be at a party and someone else's wife gives me "come-on" signals. When I show interest and she backs off, she is playing a game. She has derived the satisfaction of knowing that she can still "hook" a man, at her age, but she has achieved this at my expense.

A great deal of material has been written about games which are usually destructive and which most people play to a greater or lesser extent depending on their own feelings of self-esteem. I do not wish to belabor the concept of games because they have been adequately dealt with in such books as *Games People Play* by Eric Berne and many others. The aim of the individual in attempting to develop the "I'm O.K. — You're O.K." life position should be to live a game-free existence without ulterior motive and without psychological kicks at the expense of others.

I would like to note in passing, however, that people tend to pick and stay with certain games throughout their lives and not only that but to adopt the same role in each game. In the game "alcoholic", the victim may drink, not just to get drunk for the sake of getting drunk, but so that his wife will persecute him and the priest, doctor, or A.A. will rescue him. If the alcoholic dies or leaves his wife it is not uncommon, in fact it tends to be the rule, that the wife will pick another husband who is an alcoholic so that she can continue playing her role in the game. There is one pair of marriage games which I would like to mention. It occurs so often that I think we should be made aware of it. The one partner usually plays the game of "kick me" in which he/she deliberately does things to annoy the spouse or continuously nags in order to get negative strokes rather than none at all. The other partner usually responds by withdrawal (or using the "silent treatment"). This is a vicious circle and causes the relationship to deteriorate until both start considering games involving other sexual partners. Divorce Court here we come! Games are, therefore, designed to fulfill the needs of the Child, even if the recognition so obtained is unpleasant. In other words, "bad" strokes are better than no recognition at all. The same could be said to apply to the naughty boy who deliberately provokes his parents in order to get spanked.

5. **Withdrawal.** Another method of structuring time is by withdrawal. I can daydream, and this is not necessarily a bad thing, provided I don't do too much of it. I can also withdraw in the more pathological sense of cutting myself off from reality, in which case I will receive no strokes at all and, therefore, my feelings about myself will tend to be "Not O.K.".

6. **Intimacy.** The final way in which I can structure my time is with intimacy. This is a state of affairs in which it is not necessary to say or do anything. Sometimes, with a certain few people and for relatively short periods of time, it is not necessary to perform rituals, pastimes, activities or games. Sometimes you feel just right with another person. These periods of intimacy do not last long and we do not have them with very many people. You may be walking along the beach holding the hand of someone you love or watching a sunset or listening to a favorite piece of music.

However, there is a snag attached to intimacy. In order to be intimate with another person it is necessary for that person to know you. You cannot be intimate with a stranger. This involves a degree of risk because if I let you know me *as I am*, then I have to let you know those areas in which I am a slob. You may then laugh at me and "put me down" or gossip about me or blackmail me, depending upon what I tell you of myself. Most of us, therefore, tend to avoid intimacy because we are too frightened to let another human being close enough to us to really know us. I would like at this point to recommend a book by Sidney M. Jourard called *The Transparent Self*, which goes into much greater detail in this respect. When I first read this book, I felt that he was recommending pretty strong medicine. I have since found that if I risk myself, if I let myself become transparent; it is a most rewarding experience, in that I have never yet been "put down", but have learned to know people more intimately than I would ever have expected to be possible.

Drives of the Child Ego State

The drives of the Child are all the instinctual drives, including self-preservation, pleasure, the preservation of the species and the drive for the fulfillment of your potential, which Abraham Maslow called "Self-Actualization". The Child, therefore, has all our mischief, spontaneity, fun, creativity, ambition, drive, and it is the powerhouse of the whole personality — the dynamo which makes the whole personality work. But as well as having all the drives it also has all the feelings and the needs of the personality and so the Child part of the personality is the vulnerable part. If the feelings are going to be "O.K." the needs must be fulfilled. If the needs are not fulfilled the feelings of the Child are going to be "Not O.K.".

I like to think of the Child as a sort of balance. If my needs are fulfilled, my feelings about myself are going to be "O.K.". If my needs are not fulfilled, I am going to feel "Not O.K.". Therefore, if I am feeling "Not O.K." about myself I have to ask myself in what way my needs are not being fulfilled; and the needs which I feel are most important are:
(1) Activities which will give me feelings of competence
(2) Intimacy which will give me feelings of significance in the eyes of others.

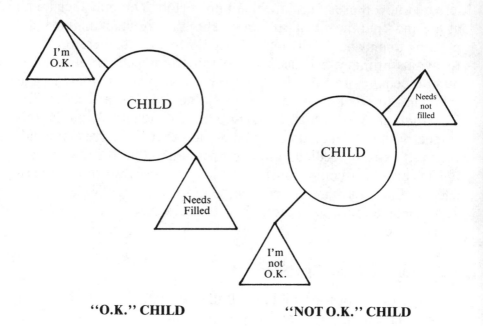

Fig. 2-2. Child as Balance of Feelings and Needs

THE PARENT

The Parent is nothing but a tape recorder. It is switched on at birth and for the first five or six years of life it records everything your parents or other authority-figures say or do. It has no feelings nor reason. It just records and plays back exactly as it recorded, without any editing or changing, without regard to fact or reality. We have all experienced watching our own children playing with their dolls and mimicking us exactly, not only with regard to what we said to them but also their tone of voice, their attitude, their stance, their mannerisms, their gestures. They are playing back to their doll exactly what we recorded in their Parent.

The Parent ego state can be divided into two parts. In one half is recorded the punishing Parent and in the other half is recorded the nurturing Parent. Into the punishing Parent go all the messages

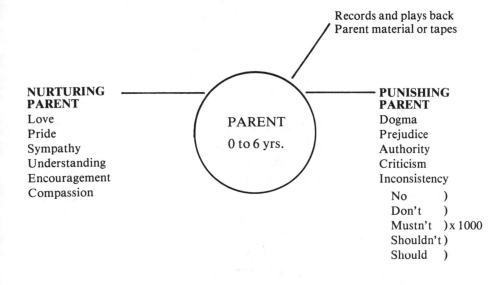

Records and plays back
Parent material or tapes

NURTURING PARENT
Love
Pride
Sympathy
Understanding
Encouragement
Compassion

PARENT
0 to 6 yrs.

PUNISHING PARENT
Dogma
Prejudice
Authority
Criticism
Inconsistency

No   )
Don't   )
Mustn't   ) x 1000
Shouldn't)
Should   )

Fig. 2-3. The Parent

relating to dogma, prejudice, authority, criticism, inconsistency and thousands of no's, don'ts, mustn'ts, and shouldn'ts.

Dogma. This is a belief which I cannot prove, such as Heaven, Hell, God, the Devil, etc. This I must either accept or reject.

Prejudice. This is a belief which has not been subjected to the light of reason and if so subjected, would prove to be wrong. For example, "It is wrong to play ball on a Sunday", "The younger generation is not worth a damn", "When I was young everybody had a sense of duty which is sorely lacking today." If these statements are examined, they are found to be untrue.

Authority as expressed by the Parent would be "Do as I say" without any reasons being given.

Inconsistency would be in telling your child not to smoke or drink while lighting a cigarette yourself. This would be recorded as "Daddy is inconsistent, so I can be inconsistent when I grow up." One of the most common inconsistencies is when we drive our car ten miles per hour above the speed limit with our children in the car. When they are sixteen, we hand them the keys of the car and say, "Now, son, drive carefully and keep within the speed limits."

Criticism, if founded upon a value judgment, would be parental, for example, "Your hair is too long" (by whose standards?).

Indignation. "You are letting the family down" (to whom and how?).

Into the nurturing Parent go all the love, pride, sympathy, understanding, encouragement and compassion which we receive from our parents and which we will, hopefully, store and replay to our own children. If a child is brought up in a foster home or orphanage and does not record these tapes he may have great difficulty in showing love to his own children.

Also recorded in the Parent are all those things which we have learned from our parents which are not really related to fact and reality but which are messages which have been handed down to us as facts and which we have not tested against reality. All these messages are going to be played back at some time in the future, with high fidelity, and they are going to be played back either to hurt our own Child or to hurt somebody else's Child.

The Parent ego state is the result of what Berne would call "scripting" and is like a script in the play of life in which you are expected to live in accordance with your parents' or other significant authoritative person's beliefs with regard to your life.

The function of the Parent ego state is therefore, to establish a value system for the person. Whether this value system is "good", "bad" or conflicting depends upon the amount and nature of the material recorded, and whether the material recorded from your mother is consistent with that from your father. The Parent ego state develops rapidly from shortly after birth until about six years of age, when, although it does not stop completely, it slows down in its recording of parental material because by this time the third part of the Ego or personality, The Adult, is now accumulating sufficient data to make valid judgments with regard to some of the incoming Parent data. Unfortunately, this process of maturation of the Adult reason is a slow one and an incomplete one and therefore, some (and often many) incorrect values are established because of the immaturity of the critical faculty of the developing Adult reason.

The Parent ego state stays with us all our lives but it should be relegated to the status of an archaic appendage. If it is allowed to rule over our total personality, then we are subjugating ourselves for life; we are becoming the puppets of our parents (even though long dead), and we cannot be free, honest, rational, creative persons, but must be content to live and die according to a prescribed pattern laid down for us by others.

THE ADULT

At the age of about one, the third part of the personality begins to develop. This is called the Adult. It is basically divided into two parts — reason and memory. The function of the Adult is to examine facts and reality in the outside world. It reasons, explores, tests, criticizes, compares, computes, contrasts, weighs, measures, calculates, updates and stores. It also controls the personality as a whole. It begins to examine the dogma, prejudice, criticism, authority and inconsistency of the Parent to see if these are true, and it has to keep re-evaluating these beliefs to see if they are as true today as they were last week, last year or forty years ago. I was brought up with tapes such as "You mustn't play with the boys down the road because they are Protestants", "It is a sin to eat meat on a Friday", and it was even considered "sinful" for my mother to knit on Sundays!

I remember attending a wedding when I was about forty-five years old. Half way through the service I started to fidget and was wishing they would get on with it so that we could get to the reception and the champagne. I suddenly realized that my parents were manipulating me, from their graves, like a puppet on strings, with a recording which they had made forty years before which said "It is a mortal sin to attend a Protestant service", and my Parent was making my Child feel bad.

If Parent information is examined by the reason of the Adult and found to be true, it is stored in the Parent part of the Adult memory bank for future use. If it is found to be untrue, then it is rejected. In this way, hopefully, those characteristics of the Parent dealing with love, pride, sympathy, encouragement, permissiveness and consistency (the nurturing parents) will be examined and having been found valid, will be stored for future use to enable us

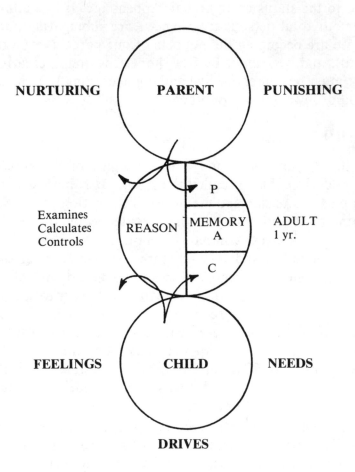

Fig. 2-4. The Adult

to become good parents in our turn. However, any Parent material such as the prejudiced statements like — "all foreigners are bad", or "all non-believers are damned", or "it is a sin to eat meat on a Friday", are found to be untrue and rejected.

At the same time, the reason of the Adult begins to examine the feelings, needs, and drives of the Child to see if they are appropriate now. If I am standing in the middle of the freeway and there are three lines of traffic coming at me and I do not feel anxious, then there is something wrong with me. Anxiety is, therefore, a reasonable Child feeling and should be used. Get on the sidewalk!

If, however, I am sitting at home and feeling as anxious as if there were three lines of traffic coming at me, then this is an unreasonable feeling and should be rejected.

If the feelings, needs and drives of the Child ego state are fulfilled in an appropriate manner, and these, after examination by the reason of the Adult, are incorporated into the Child portion of the memory bank of the Adult as appropriate Child feelings, drives and needs, then we have gone a long way towards building a healthy Adult.

All this time, the growing Adult is examining facts and storing them for future use. For example, a child may play with matches and find that he gets burned. This is a fact which he has found out for himself. He knows it to be true. Nobody told him to accept this fact. He tested it for himself and it is stored in his Adult memory bank as information which he has established for himself. A child may see a car coming and run across the road in front of it and nearly get run over. He may then think, "Next time I see a car coming at that speed I'm going to let it go." He is beginning to learn to judge distance and speed. These facts have to be constantly tested against the reality of the now to see if they are still true. The child who played with matches and got burned should not grow up to think that matches are "bad" when he is older. This means that a constant re-evaluation or updating of the material stored in the Adult memory bank is necessary to maintain a state of psychological health.

Throughout his life the Adult ego must constantly re-examine the feelings, drives and needs of the Child to see if they are appropriate, true and useful. If so, he incorporates them; if not he rejects them. In this way the archaic Child is "shrunken" and the healthy, reasonable Child in the Adult is enlarged, so that in the healthy personality the archaic Child ego is no longer able to achieve executive control of the whole personality. In the same way the dogma and prejudice and all the other parental material is constantly being examined to see if it is still true, in which case, it is incorporated. If it is not, it is rejected. In this way, the archaic Parent ego state is "shrunken" so that it can no longer take control of the personality and yet those characteristics of the nurturing Parent which are going to enable that person to be a healthy, adequate parent, are preserved in the Parent part of the Adult ego state.

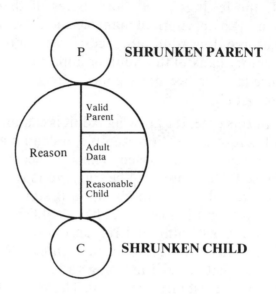

Fig. 2-5. The Healthy Personality

THE EFFECTS OF THE ENVIRONMENT ON THE GROWING PERSONALITY

During the process of maturation, our Child is subjected to many and varied influences, as follows:

The parent who does a lot of saying, "No", "Don't make a noise", "Don't bring dirty shoes into the house", "Don't throw your coat on the floor", "Don't leave your toys in the living room", "Don't be late for supper", "Don't come in after dark", or "Wait until tomorrow", "Don't let the family down".

The school. There they say, "No chewing gum in class", "No talking in class", "No playing in the corridor", "You must conform".

The church. And what is the message which was most constantly heard in church? "Thou shalt not . . ." Thou shalt not gratify any of your "sinful" desires. We heard very little of the "Thou shalts", although this is changing.

The State gets into the act when you go out onto the highway and you are told "No speeding", "No liquor", "Stop", "Yield", "30 miles per hour", "No minors". I have yet to meet a policeman who says "Be my guest, have a race". One of my fondest memories is of motoring in Montana before the 55 miles per hour speed limit was enforced. Whenever I saw a sign reading "speed reasonable and prudent", I really felt good. I don't think I ever had the urge to speed in Montana, which I always have everywhere else.

The peer group. As a person grows further they tend to begin to separate themselves from parents, school, church, and to lean more heavily upon their peer group, which begins to assume great importance and youngsters are subjected to great pressure from their peer group, usually expressed in the form of "You mustn't be a square", "You must smoke", "You must drink", "You mustn't have your hair cut", "You're not going to be in at 10 o'clock are you?", "You're not going to do what your parents tell you are you?".

Society. This adds a lot of pressure in the form of standards, manipulations and traps, such as: "conform", "produce", "You must keep up with the Jones's". When people try to manipulate you, this makes you feel bad, particularly if they are successful. And very often we find ourselves in traps, possibly of our own making, such as mortgage payment traps, marriage traps, business partnership traps, morality traps, cultural traps, and we feel frustrated because we do not know how to get out of the traps or we are unwilling to pay the price involved.

Unfinished business. Problems which are unresolved but which are pushed into the background and "clutter up" the subconscious, causing chronic low-grade tension.

Internal Parent. To add to all of this, as if this were not enough, there is the influence of one's own Parent tapes, saying "Don't play with yourself", "No masturbation", "No sex before marriage", "Boys don't cry", "Nice girls don't drink alone in public", "Don't let the family down".

As a result of all these repressive influences, the poor, free, fun-loving mischievous, creative, spontaneous Child gets squashed.

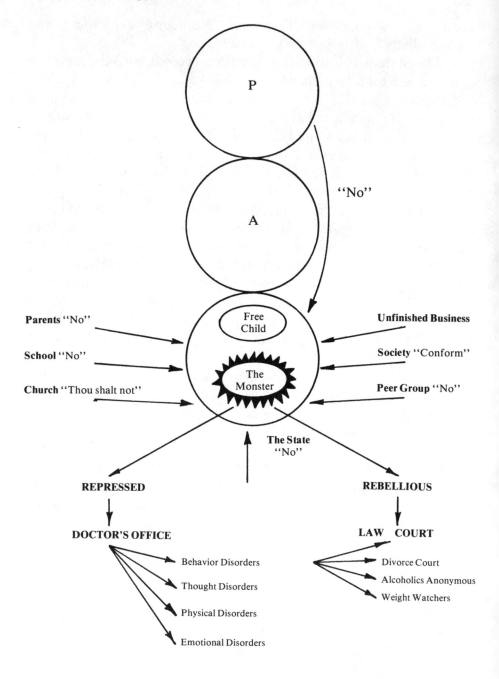

Fig. 2-6 The Formation of the Monster

It feels that every time it expresses any feelings somebody is going to clobber it. As a result the remainder of the Child becomes adapted. We all have to be adapted to a certain extent in order to live in civilization. I cannot empty garbage on your living room floor or knock you down and steal your wallet, but if I become over-adapted and I keep within me feelings which I should express, then those repressed feelings will create what I call the Monster in my Child, and this Monster is going to destroy me if it can. It will eat me up. And it will destroy me in one of two ways. Either it will make me Rebellious, in which case I may run amuck, break the law, hold up a gas station, be arrested by the police and end up in the Law Courts, or I may become Repressed and keep all my feelings to myself, in which case I may end up in the doctor's office with one of four types of conditions:

1. **Emotional disorders** (anxiety, depression, phobias, compulsions).

2. **Physical disorders** (migraine headaches, tension headaches, stomach or duodenal ulcers, hypertension, angina, asthma, eczema, nervous colitis, low back pain, period pains).

3. **Thought disorders.** I may decide the pressures of the outside world are so intense and distasteful that I will retreat into a world of fantasy and I will decide to become crazy. I will shut out the real world and will live in my own world of hallucinations and delusions.

4. **Behavior disorders.** I may find that when I go to work my boss "puts me down". I don't know how to cope with the situation so I become aggressive in my driving and come in conflict with the law. I may take out my repressions in an extra-marital affair and find myself facing a divorce. I may smoke or drink to excess or look for solace in drugs.

So you can see the *Monster in my Child* has an immense power to destroy me if I will allow it.

We, therefore, tend to surround ourselves with a primitive shell, armor or capsule which we think will defend us from the repressive influences of the outside world. And it does, to some extent, fulfill this task in that some of the repressive influences are warded off. But, unfortunately, this shell prevents us from fulfilling the needs of our Child which are for stimulation, recognition and

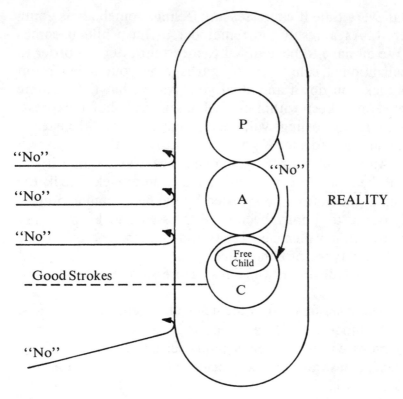

Fig. 2-7 Blocking Awareness with the Capsule

intimacy because it cuts us off from the world of reality. Also, reality being outside the capsule, our Parent ego tapes cannot be reality-tested and therefore, our Parent ego state can have a "field day" with our Child and make it feel very bad.

I have sometimes observed a person walking down the street on a beautiful summer day. They are obviously well fed and well clothed. They are apparently physically well. There is nobody chasing them with a knife or a gun. And yet they look utterly miserable. They are unaware of the fact that the sun is shining, that the trees and flowers have beautiful colors, that their circumstances in life are really very fortunate. They are living within their capsule. They are unaware of the reality of the now.

Fritz Perls, the originator of the Gestalt movement, said the difference between the past and the present is guilt and depression. If I live in the past I am going to feel guilty or depressed. The difference between the future and the present is anxiety. If I live in the future I am going to be anxious about where my mortgage payments are going to come from, how my children are going to grow up, what is going to happen to the economic situation in the world, etc., etc., and I am going to feel anxious. It is only in the now that I can be truly happy.

Sometimes I will have a patient sitting in my office and the following type of exchange will occur:

Me: "What are you aware of now?"

Patient: "I have had a terrible week."

Me: "That was last week. What are you aware of now?"

Patient: "We are entertaining six guests for supper tonight and I have to go to the stores on the way home."

Me: "No. That is in half an hour. What are you aware of now?"
This may be followed by a considerable silence, so I may do some prompting:

Me: "Are you aware of the green carpet on the floor?"

Patient: "Oh, yes."

Me: "Are you aware of the fan in the air conditioning?"

Patient: "Yes."

Me: "Are you aware of the chair you are sitting in?"

Patient: "Yes indeed. It is very comfortable."

Me: "Are you feeling embarrassed?"

Patient: "No."

Me: "Are you feeling anxious?"

Patient: "No."

Me: "How are you actually feeling at this moment?"

Patient: "Fine."

They will then usually begin to laugh as they realize that, in actual fact, while they are concentrating on the facts and realities of the now, they do indeed feel fine. This is one of the major contributions of Gestalt therapy towards psychotherapy as a whole in that it does concentrate on training the patient to become aware of the now.

SOME PERSONALITY TYPES

I would like to try to describe in Transactional terms some of the common personality types.

The socially over-adapted person

This is the person whose Child has been virtually squashed. He has a large Punishing Parent. Most of his Child is over-adapted. His free Child is almost non-existent and his Monster is very tightly controlled. He tends to be lacking in fun, creativity or imagination. He is dull and uninteresting at a party. He may have a good functioning Adult and feels comfortable when discussing adult topics, but he is totally incapable of making a fool of himself. He is the very antithesis of the "life and soul of the party".

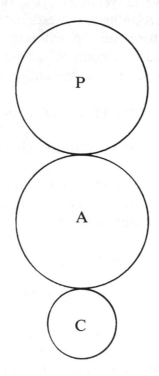

Fig. 2-8 The Socially Over-Adapted Person

Alcohol may knock out his Parent and he may be able to loosen up a little. If however, he drinks too much and this deadens his Adult, then his Monster may be turned loose and he may become ugly or amorous, but in either case he will be totally unpredictable. Drunk or sober, he is a bore.

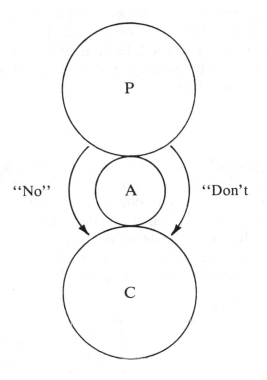

"No"   "Don't

Fig. 2-9 The Neurotic

The neurotic.

This is the person whose Parent is filled with dogmatic, pre-judiced, authoritarian, critical, inconsistent and negative tapes which lead to feelings of guilt and depression; whose Child is filled with irrational fears, unreasonable drives and needs and whose Adult is insufficiently mature to cope with these two powerful, although archaic ego states. This person is, in consequence, a puppet of his early conditioning, who is condemned to live the "script" of life given to him by those in authority over him in his early life. He has to conform to standards set by other people.

He is not a free agent. He cannot choose his own mode of life but must live as a slave. Only by "shrinking" his Parent by the careful examination and rejection of all the beliefs which are dogmatic and prejudiced; by watching himself to determine if his actions are based upon fact and reality; only by shrinking his

Child, by examining all the feelings to see if they are reasonable or appropriate or whether they are caused by excessively strong Parent tapes or by "Not O.K." feelings of his insecure Child, can he break the tyranny of his script and learn to live an autonomous life as a free human being.

The psychopath

This is generally the person who has been brought up in a number of foster homes or institutions in which the influence of the punishing Parent was very strong. He was constantly discounted and "put down", but the nurturing Parent is absent or virtually non-existent. He records little or no love, sympathy, pride, permissiveness, encouragement or recognition. As a consequence, his Child becomes rebellious and he "switches off" his Parent.

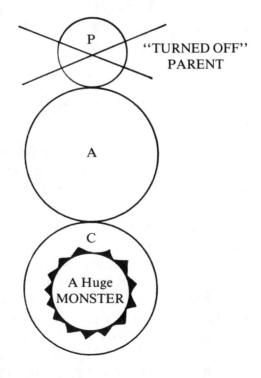

Fig. 2-10 The Psychopath

When this person grows up he may have a good-functioning Adult, with lots of factual data at his command; he may have a good intellect and may be able to manipulate people to his advantage. His rebel Child demands instant gratification of his wishes and he has no steadying influence of a functioning Parent. He will do anything which his Adult tells him he has a good chance of getting away with. This person may develop into the criminal psychopath who will shoot, kill, steal, or "con" people without the least interference by "conscience".

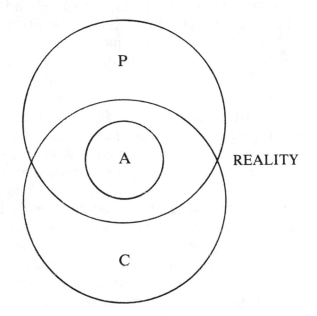

Fig. 2-11 The Psychotic

The psychotic

In the Transactional terms the psychotic is one in whom both the Parent and Child ego states are so large and there has been so much overlapping of the ego boundaries between them that they have swallowed the Adult. In this case the Adult has lost contact with reality and therefore, the person has lost contact with reality and will tend to live in a world of fantasy, fear, hallucination, delusion, guilt, anxiety, depression, or many of the myriad forms in which so-called "mental illness" can show itself.

METHODS OF TREATMENT

What can we do about this state of affairs?

1. We must dissolve the capsule and become aware of the reality of the Now. This is where the techniques of Gestalt therapy are most useful.

2. We must shrink the Parent by examining our Parent tapes, our value systems and beliefs to see if they are still as true today as they were earlier in our lives, and if not we must throw them out. This is analysis of our childhood trauma or Psycho-Analysis.

3. We must satisfy the needs of the Free Child. To do this we must follow the concepts of the Humanistic Psychologists such as: Rogers, Maslow, Coopersmith and Jourard.

4. We must express the Monster. This can be done by learned techniques of Assertiveness and by learning to cope with guilt (Behaviorism).

5. We must learn to switch off the alarm reaction to stress by Hypnosis, (T.M. or Yoga) which I class together as the "Turn-off" schools. These, however, must be backed up by all the other components if the results are going to be permanent.

6. We can learn to deal with the Rebel Child by the methods of Reality Therapy, in teaching that responsible behavior brings more satisfying and permanent rewards than can be obtained by behaving in destructive, rebellious, or anti-social ways.

7. We must use the rational approach of Transactional Analysis to integrate all of these different concepts into a practical, portable tool with which to change our lives.

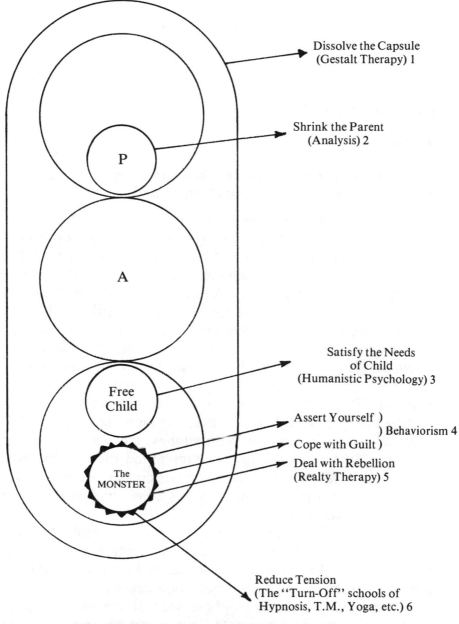

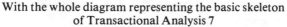

With the whole diagram representing the basic skeleton
of Transactional Analysis 7

Fig. 2-12 The Integration of Seven Theories of Psychotherapy into a Unified
Concept

3
Transactional Analysis

If two people are interacting there are six ego states involved, because each has a Parent, Adult and Child.

Complementary Transactions

If I say to you, "Where are my car keys?", this is a question dealing with fact; therefore my Adult is talking to your Adult. If you reply, "On the table behind you.", this is also a fact, therefore, your Adult is replying to my Adult. This is a Complementary Transaction, and the conversation can proceed without difficulty.

If, however, I say: "Where are my car keys?" and you reply, "I haven't got them!", you are replying with your Child to my Parent (as if to say "You are blaming me for having taken your car keys") and this is a Crossed Transaction, and the conversation ceases until we think of something else to talk about.

Because we have had a crossed transaction, we will both record a "cross" in our Monster; and these crosses are stored and saved up, like trading stamps or ammunition for the next battle between us. When we have saved up ten crosses, we may have a temper tantrum, with fifty, we may get drunk, and with five hundred we may get a divorce.

If I say, "Where are my car keys?", and you reply, "You are *always* losing your things.", you are answering my Adult-Adult stimulus with a Parent-Child response, and once again this is a crossed transaction and the conversation ceases.

Therefore, if we are to avoid crossed transactions, we must be able to recognize which ego state I am in and which ego state you are in at any given time.

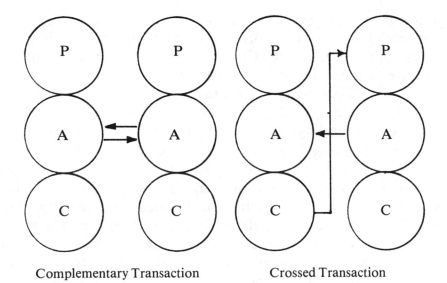

Complementary Transaction   Crossed Transaction

Fig. 3-1 Complementary and Crossed Transactions

CHARACTERISTICS OF THE EGO STATES

If we are to use Transactional Analysis as a functional tool instead of an academic theory or (worse still) a parlor game, we must be very familiar with the characteristics of the different ego states so that we can recognize them instantly, both in ourselves and other people.

The Parent

The Parent ego state shows itself by the use of such words as always, never, don't ever, how many times, the younger generation, once and for all, when I was your age; and such gestures as the wagging finger, furrowed brow, pursed lips, tut tut, sighing, and most of all, by the tone of voice.

The Child

The Child generally feels insecure and therefore, tends to boast, lie and exaggerate. It uses words like — bigger, better, best — "My Daddy is bigger than your Daddy," "My toy is better than your toy.", "I caught a fish this long." If you hear a person who is obviously boasting, lying, or exaggerating you know he is in his Child ego state; he is approximately six years old; he is feeling too insecure to admit he caught a fish only two inches long. In the same way, if a person is having a temper tantrum this denotes that he is in his Child ego state, he is six years old emotionally, he is trying to express feelings for which he has no rational outlet.

The Child may also swear, be destructive, weep, have quivering lips, pout, sulk, tease, fidget, giggle, be mischievous. The Child ego state is also given away very largely by tone of voice. Sometimes a patient will come into the doctor and say, "Oh doctor, I've got a terrible pain and it goes here and there and everywhere", and you can tell by the very tone of the voice that in actual fact the symptoms are probably not true and that this person is just feeling bad. Some people indicate the fun Child by the bubbly quality of their voice when you are speaking to them. Conversations with these people are always stimulating.

Recognizing the Parent and Child in Others

The important thing to realize is that if I can recognize, by certain words, gestures, tones of voice or facial expressions, that another person is in his Parent ego state, then I realize I am dealing with a six-year-old tape recorder which is replaying messages which it recorded in the first six years of his life. Having recognized this I can choose to turn off these messages and refuse to let them hurt my Child. I have stripped that person of his ability to make me feel bad.

If the substance of what he says is actually true but it is couched in the words, tones, gestures or expressions of the Parent, I can accept, with my Adult, the true facts, and act upon them if necessary. However, I can refuse to accept the implied rebuke because it is being transmitted by a Parent Tape Recorder and I will, therefore, not feel put down.

If I can recognize the Child in another person, I can be aware that he is in an emotional state of anger, insecurity, repression and can refuse to be drawn into conflict. If he is a significant person to me, I should respond with my Adult by some such rejoinder as, "I think you are upset about something. Would you like to talk about it?''. This gives him the opportunity of re-establishing Adult-Adult communication.

Once I have learned to recognize the Parent or Child ego states in another person, I have robbed that person of his ability to hurt me, to create crossed transactions and thus sow the seeds of future misunderstanding or conflict.

The Adult

For the indicators of the Adult ego state, I am going to place tone of voice right at the top of the list. This is, I think, the most important sign. If a patient comes in to me and says that he has a pain in the middle of his chest, which is worse when he exerts himself, which is relieved by rest, which sometimes goes down the left arm; and the tone of voice is right, then I had better investigate that person because he probably has coronary artery disease. The Adult uses such words as I think, I feel, it is my opinion, I disagree because . . . . ., and such fact-finding words as who, where, what, when, why, how. There are two other very important characteristics of the Adult ego state. The first is that Adult listening is *almost invariably* accompanied by intermittent eyeball contact. If you are talking to me and I am gazing out of the window, you do not know whether I am listening to you or whether I am dreaming of my summer vacation. If I am talking to you the only real indication which I have of your degree of understanding of what I say is the extent to which you follow me with your eyes.

If I suddenly lose your eyes, I know that one of two things has happened: either I have said something which you did not understand or you lost interest, in which case you have switched to your Child. On the other hand, you may have suddenly switched to your Parent — what I have said has triggered some prejudice and your Parent tape recorder has started. In both cases, I will lose contact with your Adult, and real communication will cease. I will lose contact with you, while you are Parent — encapsulated, until you have played the whole tape through. On one occasion, while talking to a lady patient of about 55 years of age, I was demonstrating how Adult gestures are always useful, Parent gestures are characteristic and Child gestures are usually obscene or funny. And as I gave her an example of an obscene Child gesture, she suddenly began to examine the leg of the chair next to her.

I paused and said somewhat thoughtfully, "You know, I think I triggered your Parent with that gesture!" She replied, "What do you mean?". So I said, "Let us examine that transaction. When I waved my fingers in the air, you thought "What a terrible thing to do, and in a doctor's office too." She looked a little bit embarrassed and said, "Yes, I was a little bit surprised." I then went on to point out to her that if I could trigger her Parent ego state, then I was able to manipulate her and make her act like a puppet controlled by her Parent tapes, even though her parent may have been dead for twenty years; that unless she examined her Parent tapes to see if they were true, she was at the mercy of anyone who wanted to "switch on" her Parent.

Another example of intermittent eyeball contact being a cardinal hallmark of Adult-Adult communication was the married couple who came to see me about their marriage. They were determined to have a divorce "because we cannot communicate". I noticed that while talking either to the wife or to the husband I had good Adult-Adult communication because we had excellent eyeball contact. I soon noticed, however, that they never looked at each other even if talking in the general direction of each other. It was as if there was a wall between them that stopped them from seeing each other but allowed them both to see me. I interrupted the dialogue to describe this wall between them which I could see, and said, "You cannot communicate on an Adult-Adult level because you do not have eyeball contact. When did you last look each other in the eyes?" There was an embarrassed silence and they then admitted with some surprise they had not looked each other in the eye for many months. I then suggested that perhaps now would be a good time to do just that — to sit and look in each other's eyes in silence for a few minutes. The husband said, "Do we have to?" I replied, "No, but it might be a good idea." So they moved their chairs until they were sitting opposite each other and sat and looked in each other's eyes for two or three minutes. Suddenly they both burst into tears. Then they reached out and held hands. Six sessions and three years later they are still married.

The reason for their lack of communication was they had not been looking at each other. They had been throwing snide remarks at each other over their shoulders, and re-establishment of eyeball contact had at least started the process of the restoration of a good Adult-Adult relationship.

Parent and Child Triggers

We, all of us, have Parent and Child triggers, which, if touched, will "trigger off" a Parent or Child reaction. If a person communicates with me in such a way as not to trigger a Parent prejudice or dogma or make my Child feel bad, then all will remain well and we can have complementary transactions. If, however, I start making vulgar signs to a 55 year old spinster, this will activate her Parent trigger and she will become Parent encapsulated, and I cannot communicate with her again until she has played through the whole tape with regard to "making rude gestures in doctor's offices".

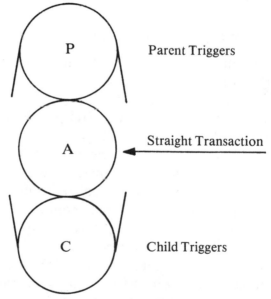

Fig. 3-2 Parent and Child Triggers

Similarly, if I upset a person's Child he will immediately become Child encapsulated and communication ceases until he becomes more reasonable.

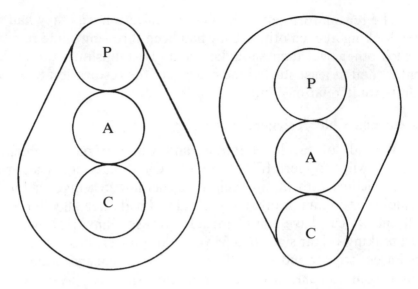

PARENT-ENCAPSULATED   CHILD-ENCAPSULATED

Fig. 3-3 Parent and Child Encapsulated Personalities

As an example, my oldest son, who is now twenty-two, cannot seem to drive his car at night without being stopped by the police and searched for alcohol. This occurs about once a week. Therefore, if I mention the word "police" I know I am going to activate his Child trigger and he will "carry on" for some time about why they always search his car and not mine and why they cannot seem to prevent serious crimes, etc., etc.

The important thing to realize is that if I can activate a Parent or a Child trigger in another person then I can manipulate him. I can either reduce him to the state of a six year old tape recorder, in which case I can predict precisely what he will say for the next ten minutes, or I can make him feel bad by reducing him to the emotional level of an insecure six year old child.

Conversely, if *my* Parent and Child triggers stick out and are obvious, anyone else *can manipulate me*, so that it is important for me to, first of all, recognize my Parent and Child triggers and then for me to cut these triggers back by the use of my Adult reason. In this way other people do not have the power to manipulate me and send me off into a Parental tirade, or trigger my Child and make me feel bad.

In other words I can and should protect my Parent and my Child with my Adult at all times. I must always ask myself if incoming stimuli are reasonable. If they are not, they are coming either from a Parent or a Child ego state, and they are designed to activate my Parent or my Child. I can therefore learn either to switch them off, or to come back with my Adult, in the hope of re-establishing good Adult-Adult communication.

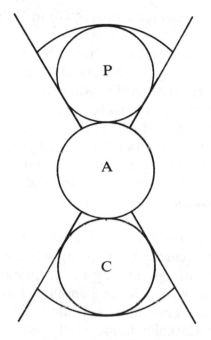

Fig. 3-4 Adult Protecting Parent and Child

Keep It Fluid

I feel that Transactional Analysis is a tool of enormous value and potential, but it must be kept flexible and must not be allowed to become too rigid, dogmatized and formalized. The important thing to recognize is whether or not you are in your Adult and whether or not the other person is in their Adult. If you are in your Parent or Child, then you are approximately six years old and behaving or thinking irrationally or irresponsibly. If he is in his

Parent or Child ego state, he is behaving or feeling irresponsibly. It is not always possible to determine whether a person is in their Parent or Child ego state because of internal dialogue. I may give a stimulus to a person's Parent and expect a Parent reply, but because of internal dialogue between his Parent and his Child, he may come back with a Child temper tantrum. Conversely, I may try to stimulate a person's Child and expect a Child reponse but instead, I may get a very Parental response:

Me: "All you Englishmen are 'stuck up' ". (Prejudiced Parent)

Him: (punching me on the nose) "Go to Hell". (Angry Child)

or

Me: (reaching for my wife) "Let's have a kiss." (Child)

Wife: "Is that *all* you think about?" (Parent)

The thing to recognize is that whatever the response, it is not within the bounds of the reasonable and is, therefore, not Adult; and there is no way that I am going to let a six year old tape recorder or a six year old child trigger either my Parent or Child into a fight on the kindergarten floor. However, it is always important for me to try to respond with my Adult to give them the chance of being reasonable and to re-establish Adult-Adult communication.

I would like, at this stage, to relate a tremendously important transaction which occurred between myself and my son when he was about 16 years of age. During the early part of his life I had brought him up with a considerable amount, I might even go so far as to say, an excessive amount of discipline. After being brought up in a fairly strict Catholic home, followed by five years in a monastery, followed by five years in the British Army, I was determined that my first son should be disciplined. In consequence, I repressed the poor little beggar almost out of existence and he had great difficulty expressing his feelings. He tended to mumble instead of speaking aloud and he tended to avoid communicating with strangers. If guests appeared at the house he would disappear. So, I began to try to undo the harm which I had done and I started to be very lax with regard to discipline. In consequence he started staying out until the early hours of the morning and I was not saying anything.

At the end of the summer holiday, when he was sixteen, I said to him, "Peter, I want you to be in by midnight for the rest of this week because school starts next week", to which he gave me no reply. About three nights later, my wife woke up at about 3 a.m. and the lights were still on downstairs. She went to check Peter's bedroom and his bed was empty. In the morning she said to me, "Peter was still out at three o'clock this morning."

Immediately this turned on my Parent tapes and I roared up to his bedroom. I was going to pull him out of bed and say, "How many times do I have to tell you to be in by midnight." Just at the door I stopped and thought, "I can't do that. It will only make his Child ego state more repressed, or more rebellious. It will give more fuel to his Monster." So, I simmered down and I went and had breakfast. After breakfast I went out to get in the car, which he had borrowed the night before, and as I opened the door of the car the smell of alcohol nearly knocked me over. Once again my Parent was turned on loud and strong and I was rushing up the stairs to drag him out of bed and say, "Haven't I told you not to have alcohol in the car?" Just at the last moment I stopped myself again. No, I cannot do that either. So, I got into the car and went off to the hospital where I fumed all morning.

At lunchtime, I came home and Peter was down, so I said, "Hi, Peter", to which he replied, "Hi, Dad". Then I said, "Was it your Adult which forgot or your rebel Child which took over last night?" After a pause and a rather queer look, he replied, "A bit of both I guess, Dad."

This was a complementary Adult-Adult transaction which had opened the lines of communication on the topic of the previous night and yet, I had not hurt his Child. I went on to say, "You know, Peter, your mother and I would dearly love to see you reach the age of about 25 without either a serious accident or a criminal record, and because of this, while you are living at home and I am supporting you, I have to lay down certain rules and regulations which you must obey. Believe me, I do not like enforcing these rules any more than you like obeying them, but I have to enforce them and you have to obey them. Because of last night, I think it is reasonable that you should lose the privilege of the car for awhile. If you accept this with your Child and have a temper tantrum and sulk, this could be for a very long time indeed. On the other hand, if you accept this as reasonable and are smiling and cheerful, then it could be for a very short time." To this he replied, "O.K., Dad." He was smiling and cheerful, and he got the car back in about two days.

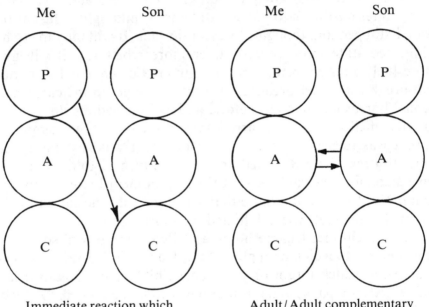

Immediate reaction which would have hurt his Child with my Parent.

Adult/Adult complementary transaction after I had cooled down. Helped to start closing the generation gap.

Fig. 3-5   Important Transaction with my Son

I feel that this was the most significant transaction that I ever had with my son. If I had used my Parent ego state in fulfilling my functions as a parent, then I would have done nothing but create an even wider generation gap. The fact that I was able to use my *Adult ego state* while performing my *functions as a parent* enabled me to close that gap and re-establish communication.

Since then I have constantly tried to promote complementary

transactions between myself and my children. For example: Adult-Adult: "What do you think we should do about this, Peter?", "What is your opinion about that Alice?", "Who is going to win the game tonight, David?" Child-Child: "Let's go shooting. Let's go swimming." Anything at which I know we can have a fun relationship together. Parent-Parent: We may grumble together about the way the teachers give so much homework at the weekend or some other prejudiced topics, but whatever it is, provided our transactions are complementary, then we are lessening the generation gap.

ORDERS OF STRUCTURAL ANALYSIS

Here we are dealing with what Eric Berne called the frontiers of structural analysis. In this we are dealing not only with the undifferentiated Parent, Adult and Child, but with what he called the differentiated ego states in which material from the Parent, the Adult and the Child of the parent are recorded in the Parent ego state; material from the Parent, Adult and Child are recorded in the Adult ego state, and material from the Parent, Adult and Child are recorded in the Child ego state.

Second Order Structural Analysis

I would now like to suggest a second order of structural analysis which is more in keeping with what I have already said. I agree with Berne that information from the parent's Parent, Adult and Child are recorded in the Parent ego state so that we can divide the Parent transversely into three segments — P.A.C. I also agree that information from the mother is recorded separately from that of the father so I am going to put a longitudinal line through the Parent to represent the father's side and the mother's side. So the final second order structural analysis of the Parent is composed of six segments which I have labelled mother Parent, mother Adult, mother Child, father Parent, father Adult and father Child.

If most of the material recorded in the Parent is recorded from the Adult portions of the mother and father, then that person will have many, many good tapes to help them to become a good reasonable parent. And if there is a lot of Child material recorded

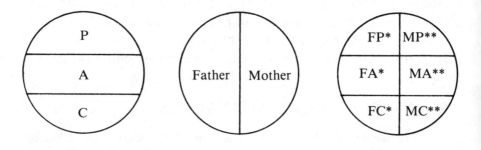

* FP — Father Parent; FA — Father Adult; FC — Father Child
** MP — Mother Parent; MA — Mother Adult; MC — Mother Child

Fig. 3-6 Second Order Structural Analysis of the Parent

in the Parent, then they may be very permissive and fun-loving, or rebellious and mischievous. If, however, most of the material is Parent, then they will be handing on a lot of scripty material, whether nurturing or punishing, depending upon the circumstances.

The second order structural analysis of the Adult is first into two parts divisible by a longitudinal line into reason and memory. The memory bank is then subdivided into three portions, the first of which is the Adult, in which is stored all that material which the Adult has been able to accumulate from the world around it, to validate with its reason and to store for future use. The other two portions are the Parent and the Child. In the Parent are recorded those Parent tapes which have been tested by reason and found true and recorded for future use, and in the Child portion of the memory bank will be those feelings, needs, and drives of the Child which have been examined by reason and found to be appropriate.

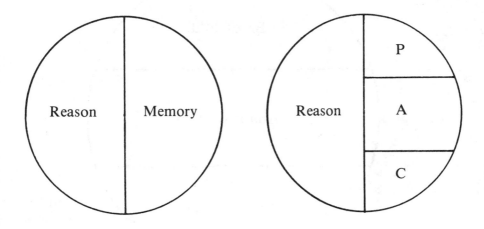

Fig. 3-7 Second Order Structural Analysis of the Adult

I cannot agree with Berne in his division of the Child ego state into Parent, Adult and Child subdivisions. The Child is the driving force of the personality. It is primitive and it doesn't record messages as such but just becomes changed by the surrounding forces, both internal and external, so that the free undifferentiated Child becomes adapted in order to conform to the rules of society because it has found that if it does not, then somebody is liable to hurt it. If the Child is subjected to very much repressive influence and keeps within it feelings which should be expressed, it becomes over-adapted and forms *the Monster* which is going to try to destroy it if it can. If there are not enough repressive influences exerted upon the Child, the free Child can also destroy us with its desire for instant gratification and pleasure *now* and it may cause us to do and say things which are inappropriate. It does not take into consideration fact and reality *now* and may do something which, although appropriate at a later date, would be inappropriate now. I would like to include within the Free Child the concept of "The Little Professor", described by James and Jongeward (12), because it has the childish ability to manipulate, to create and to be intuitive. It has not been over-adapted. It is the

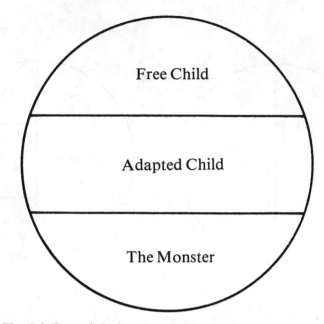

Fig. 3-8 Second Order Structural Analysis of the Child

little professor in the Child which helps the Adult to write a book, compose a song, give an inspired speech. The little professor is undoubtedly part of the Free Child.

I, therefore, feel the second order of structural analysis of the Child should be to divide it into three portions: The Free Child, the Adapted Child, and the Monster.

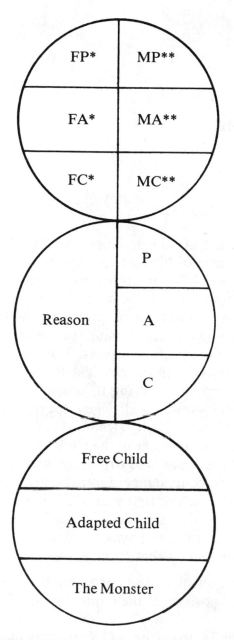

* FP — Father Parent; FA — Father Adult; FC — Father Child
** MP — Mother Parent; MA — Mother Adult; MC — Mother Child

Fig. 3-9 Complete Second Order Structural Analysis

4
Development
of the
Life
Positions

I would like to trace the development of the life positions during the first six years of life and subsequently to maturity. In the first year of life, a child's parents are not usually punishing in their attitudes and actions towards the baby. Their nurturing Parent ego state is usually at its most active, providing the love, pride, sympathy, understanding and compassion, so the child gets its "O.K." feelings from the Parent of its parents. The Adult ego state of the parent is busy supplying all the physical needs of the child, feeding it, cleaning it, warming it, drying it, protecting it. The Child ego state of the parent shows its strongest feelings of love, warmth, mischief, fun and lots of "O.K." feelings. It is not until the child is three or four that the Monster in the Child of the parent begins to show its frustration, anger, and irritability after months of broken sleep, dirty diapers, colic, temper tantrums and childish manipulation. Therefore, during this first year of life it is not surprising that the infant develops the attitude of "You're O.K." towards its parents. The fact that it is so physically dependent is inevitably going to lead to the feeling that "I'm not O.K.".

It, therefore, seems reasonable to me that the "I'm not O.K. — You're O.K." position is the natural position of every normal child.

When the child grows up and finds that most of his Parent tapes are reasonable and most of his Child feelings are ap-

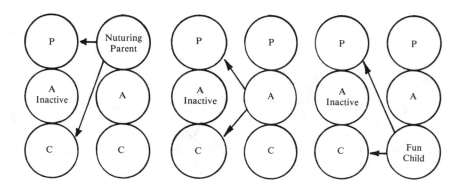

Fig. 4-1 Formation of "I'm Not O.K. — You're O.K." Position

propriate, then he will tend to develop as a well-integrated personality who will be better prepared to face the pressures and conflicts of the outside world.

After the First Year

After this initial period, when the Adult of the developing child is beginning to function, things begin to change. Some of the Parent tapes become punishing, some of the Child messages become hurtful due to the Monster in the Child of the parent. In this way, many different attitudes can be adopted. In this period, when the Adult is beginning to function more efficiently, it begins to intercept and evaluate the incoming information; and to make decisions as to whether "I'm O.K." or "Not O.K." or "You're O.K." or "You're Not O.K.". By the time the child is about six years old its Parent ego state is almost fully formed and its Adult is beginning to protect its Parent and Child by the use of reason.

If most of the Parent tapes are punishing and the Child tapes inconsistent, then the position "I'm Not O.K. — You're Not O.K." may develop. If the punishing Parent is so strong that the growing child "turns off the Parent" and protects its Child with its Adult, then the "I'm O.K. — You're not O.K." position may develop.

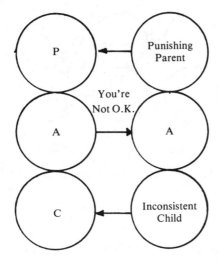 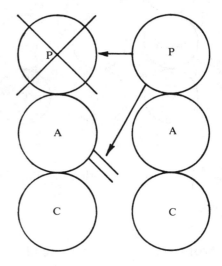

"I'm Not O.K. — You're Not O.K."   "I'm O.K. — You're Not O.K."

Fig. 4-2 Formation of "I'm Not O.K. — You're Not O.K." and "I'm O.K. — You're Not O.K." Positions

If most of the data in the Parent ego state proves on examination by the Adult to be true and reasonable and most of the Child feelings are found to be good feelings, then the individual will grow up to be a well adjusted person with an "I'm O.K. — You're O.K." position.

Dr. T. Harris suggests there are four life positions:
1. "I'm not O.K. — You're O.K."

This is the position of every child at birth. It is pushed out of a warm, comfortable womb, onto a cold, slippery, wet caseroom table, its bottom is smacked, it is put into a crib where it can't turn over, scratch its nose, feed itself or change its diaper. It is totally dependent upon the nurse or its mother and it feels "I'm not O.K. — You're O.K.".

2. "I'm not O.K. — You're not O.K."

This is the position of the child when he finds that his parents are inconsistent and cannot be relied upon, when most of his incoming data is from the Child of his parents.

3. "I'm O.K. — You're not O.K."

This is the position adopted when the child is so mistreated that the only time he feels O.K. is when he is left alone. This occurs four or five times every hour in the United States when a child is beaten by his own parent so badly that he has fractured skull or broken ribs. The child may be lying there keeping his head still and breathing very shallowly and he thinks to himself "I'm O.K. as long as I don't breathe too deeply and don't move my head." Then he sees his mother coming to pick him up and thinks "Keep away from me, because if you pick me up my ribs will hurt or my head will hurt", and he thinks "I'm O.K. as long as *you* leave me alone", or "I'm O.K. — You're not O.K."

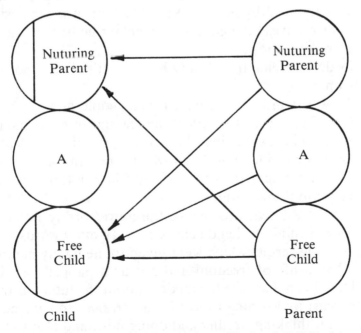

Fig. 4-3 Formation of "I'm O.K. — You're O.K." Position

4. "I'm O.K. — You're O.K."

This is the healthy position in life in which the person has changed his own "Not O.K." feelings to "O.K." feelings about himself. It is a position that has to be adopted and occurs only if the needs of the Child for stimulation, recognition and structure are fulfilled.

Harris then goes on to say that it is the Christian position. I must admit, when I first saw that, I took it with a pinch of salt. I could not at the time equate the "I'm O.K. — You're O.K." position with being meek and humble of heart and turning the other cheek, but I made a note of it. I shall return to this later because it is rather interesting.

Dr. Harris believes that the first three positions, once adopted, tend to remain fixed throughout life unless special efforts are directed to changing them. I personally feel, from my own experience, that in the early stages of life we may fluctuate through all these positions, possibly many times, but that we will gradually decide upon a predominant stance or position. However, I agree that the "I'm O.K. — You're O.K." position is the position of the psychologically healthy person. Not only that, it is the position of the person who lives "the good life" whether he be Christian, Jew, Moslem or Agnostic.

How do I develop the "I'm O.K. — You're O.K." position? It depends upon —

1. How I communicate with other people now.

2. How I can learn to express the feelings of my Child in such a way that while expressing these feelings I do not react with irresponsible behavior or feelings which are irrational.

3. How I can feed the needs of my Child in terms of stimulation, recognition, and intimacy.

4. How I can learn to reduce the power of my Parent tapes over the way I think, feel and behave now. In other words, how can I reject any life scripts which were given to me by my parents and begin to live a life of freedom and not as a puppet?

5. How I can decrease the anxiety about the future or the guilt about the past by learning to live in the *present*; to become aware of what I am thinking, feeling and doing now; and also to become aware of the ways in which I have developed a block to awareness.

TYPES OF TRANSACTIONS

I would like to amplify, briefly, the different types of transactions and to point out those areas in which I feel I have to differ from Berne.

The Complementary Transaction

This is a stimulus from one ego state which evokes a response from an appropriate ego state in the other person such as to facilitate or encourage further transactions.

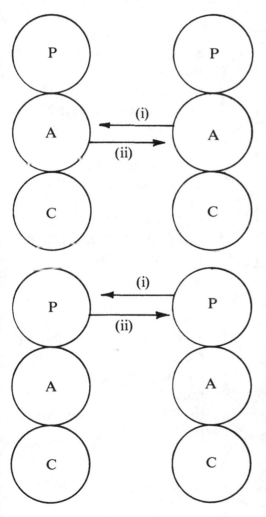

1. Complementary Adult-Adult
(i) "Where are my car keys?"
(ii) "In your top drawer."
Note that these are both rational statements — one asking for information and the other supplying it.

2. Complementary Parent-Parent
(i) "Children are all the same."
(ii) "Yes. They never have any respect for their elders!"
Note that both these statements are prejudiced and do not stand up to the light of reason. But these two people can have a very happy "beef" about the state of the world for as long as they like.

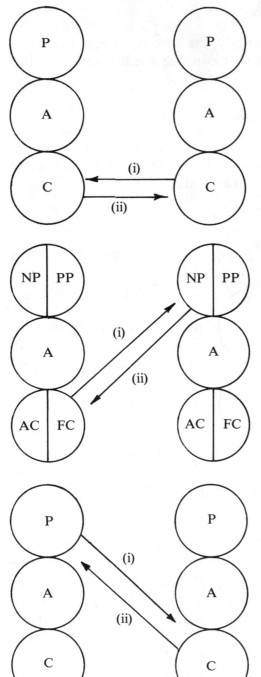

3. Complementary Child-Child

(i) "Let's take those apples."

(ii) "Oh yes, I love apples." Once again, this sort of conversation can continue indefinitely while they both remain in their Child ego states.

4. Complementary Child-Parent

(i) "Mommy I banged my knee and it feels terrible."

(ii) "Let Mommy kiss it better."

This occurs when the free Child transacts with the nurturing Parent, but as we shall see later all Parent-Child transactions are not complementary.

5. Complementary Parent-Child

(i) "Mommy loves you very much."

(ii) "I love you too, Mommy."

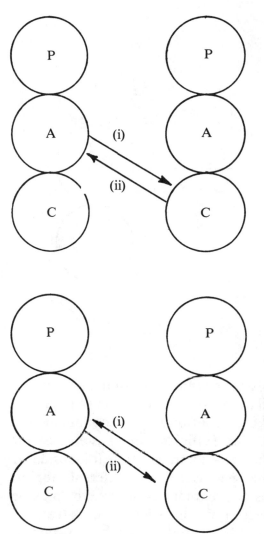

6. Complementary Adult-Child

(i) "Let me make you more comfortable."

(ii) "It's nice being sick because everyone is so kind to me."

(This could be non-verbal)

7. Complementary Child-Adult

(i) "I want to go out and play."

(ii) "Yes dear, when you have finished your breakfast."

Berne believed there were nine sets of complementary transactions, but I do not feel it is possible to have a complementary transaction between the Parent and the Adult. If a Parent stimulus is received by the Adult, the Adult will tend to act in a rational way and the response will be towards the Adult of the other and thus the lines will not be parallel, for example,

(i) "These buses are always late."

(ii) "It is 10:40. We should be on time."

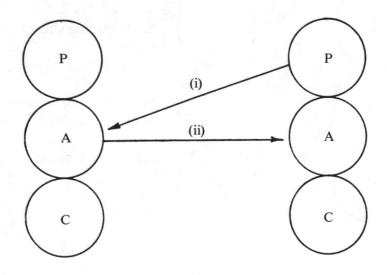

Crossed Transactions

A crossed transaction is one in which the stimulus from one ego state to another is crossed by a response between two other ego states in such a way that the conversation *stops*. Communication ceases, at least on that topic, until sufficient time has elapsed for the hostility generated by the crossed transaction to subside or further transactions become necessary on different topics. Whichever of these conditions or eventualities occurs, you may be certain that the crossed transaction will have left its mark (call it a cross or trading stamp) in the Monster of the Child ego state of both parties involved, and unless this crossed transaction is *uncrossed immediately*, these crosses will be saved up to be used later, like ammunition for the next battle. The inference to be drawn from this is that crossed transactions are to be avoided at all cost. If they occur, either by accident or design, they must be uncrossed *right now* by the determined use of the Adult ego state to ensure that no hard feelings remain in the Monster of the Child which may be stored up as a future weapon to justify irresponsible behavior.

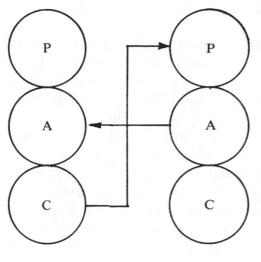

1. "I can't find the tool box."
2. "I didn't move it."
This represents an Adult-Adult stimulus being crossed by a Child-Parent response and the conversation ceases. In this case a simple Adult-Adult statement dealing with fact and reality is replied to by a Child-Parent response as if to say "You are blaming me for having left the tool box in the wrong place."

The first person feels annoyed and frustrated because he has been misunderstood. The second person feels hurt and frustrated because he thinks he is being blamed unjustly. *The conversation stops.* Both of them then record a cross in the Monster in their Child. If this is allowed to stay without being resolved or un-crossed, the seeds have been sown for a future conflict out of all proportion to the triviality of the incident. When one party or the other has saved up enough ammunition to "blow his top" the manner in which he expresses his pent-up feelings will be the result of 30 or 40 trivial crossed transactions, which were not uncrossed at the time, and will, therefore, be totally unreasonable, unacceptable and misunderstood. It will tend to compound the injury and lead the parties further and further apart in their quest for the ultimate in transactions, i.e., intimacy.

How does one uncross a crossed transaction? In the example above it means that the person asking the question must resolutely refuse to accept a cross in his Child due to the misinterpretation of his question and must *stick to his Adult* in a second transaction to clear the misunderstanding, for example, "I know you didn't move it, but I was wondering aloud as to where it could be." In this case the lines of communication are open again, further conversation may ensue on either this or any other topic, and neither party records or stores a cross or trading stamp for ammunition in the Monster of his Child.

This reminds me of a crossed transaction I had with my wife last winter. It was very cold when I came home one evening. I hung up my coat in the hall and went to sit in the living room. Suddenly I thought, "By gosh, it's cold in here," and I looked up and saw that I had left the inside door open. I got up to close the door and was walking towards it when I suddenly realized that my wife had been going around opening doors and windows recently because of her hot flushes. My wife was in the kitchen so I said, "Would you like me to leave the door open, Love?" Her immediate response was, "I didn't leave it open." My automatic reaction was to let my Child slam the door, turn up the TV and not speak to her the rest of the evening. Then I realized this wouldn't do, and so I said, "I know you didn't leave the door open. I left it open, but because you have been going around opening all the doors and windows recently, I thought perhaps you might like it open." "Oh no, I'm fine," she replied and started to laugh. "Did you realize that you had crossed the transaction?", I said. "Yes, it's easy isn't it," she replied. Now, it may seem that this was a lot of trouble to go to to uncross that transaction and that I had to stick to my Adult with great determination in order to do so, but if you can learn to do this it will certainly pay off.

Another way of dealing with crossed transactions is to ignore them. One can refuse to accept a cross in your Monster on the grounds that the response is coming from a Child ego state which is immature and loaded with trading stamps and intellectually about six years old, feeling very insecure; or coming from a Parent ego state which is nothing but the replaying of recordings made in the other's Parent ego state before the age of six.

In neither case is he going to allow them to hurt his Child. He may, therefore, say nothing and leave the transaction crossed, but in this case, even if he emerged from the transaction unscathed, his partner will not, and he may be sowing seeds of future trouble especially if the person concerned is one whose significance is important to him, such as a wife, child, mother or close friend.

There is another form of crossed transaction which I feel has not been sufficiently stressed in the literature, but which, to my mind, causes much ill-will and misunderstanding between parents and children. This is, in my opinion, one of the greatest causes of the "generation gap". I refer to crossed transactions between the Parent and the Child ego states. When you realize that the Parent has two distinct sides: punishing and nurturing; and the Child may have three: free Child, adapted Child and Monster, then you can see the possibilities for misunderstanding and blocks to intimacy.

Punishing Parent-Monster Crossed Transaction

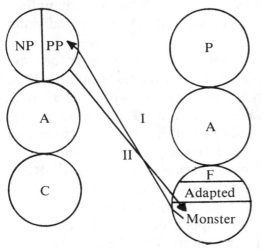

(i) "How many times do I have to tell you to wipe your feet when you come in?"
(ii) "You don't have to shout!"

Monster-Punishing Parent Crossed Transaction

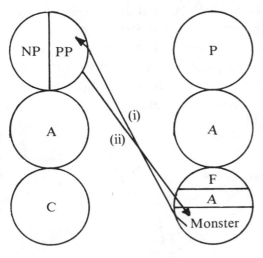

(i) "Where the hell is my supper?"
(ii) "Don't you ever talk to me in that way. Wait your turn."

Punishing Parent-Adapted Child Crossed Transaction

Parent: "How many times do I have to tell you to be in by midnight?"

Child: Saying nothing — thinks — "Hell, why does he always pick on me?" He becomes more repressed and uncommunicative.

Adapted Child-Punishing Parent Crossed Transaction

Child: Mumbles something unintelligible.

Parent: "Why don't you speak up? You are always mumbling. How can you expect anyone to understand you if you don't speak up!"

As you can see, crossed Transactions in any shape or form are the cause of failure in inter-personal transactions and must be avoided. To achieve intimacy in our relations with others, to be autonomous and to live an adult life free from the puppet strings attached to us by our parents and other authority figures, to be free from the role playing and script following which so many of us allow to gum up our lives, we must learn to stick to the Adult ego state. Only by staying in our Adult can we be free, self-directing, growing, maturing, actualizing human beings. If we stay in our Child or Parent ego states we are puppets of our early experiences and suggestions with all that they entail. The choice is ours!

Non-Complementary Transactions

This is a type of transaction which has not hitherto been dealt with in that it is not complementary and therefore encouraging further transactions; neither is it crossed, therefore, blocking further transactions. The non-complementary transaction changes the direction of the transaction without either facilitating it or stopping it. It usually involves four ego states.

Non-Complementary Parent-Parent/Adult-Adult

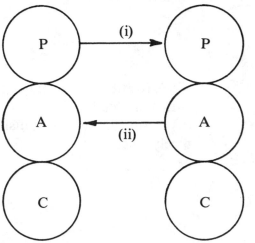

(i) "These airplanes are always late."
(ii) "I make it 9:30. We should be on time."

Non-Complementary Adult-Adult/Parent-Parent

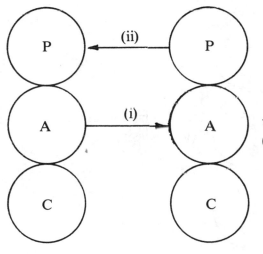

(i) "Our plane should be on time."
(ii) "For a change."

Non-Complementary Parent-Parent/Child-Child

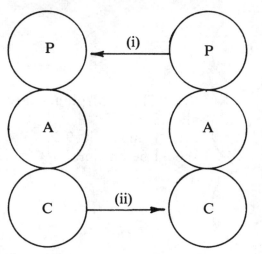

(i) "How disgusting playing with that mud."
(ii) "But doesn't it squish nicely between your fingers?"

Non-Complementary Child-Child/Parent-Parent

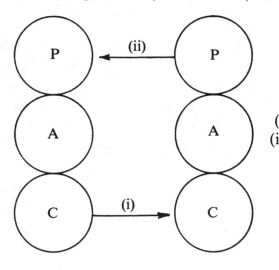

(i) "Kiss me again."
(ii) "Kissing is sinful."

Non-Complementary Adult-Adult/Child-Child

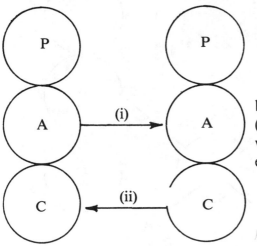

(i) "How far away is that boat?"
(ii) "You look beautiful when you screw up your eyes."

Non-Complementary Child-Child/Adult-Adult

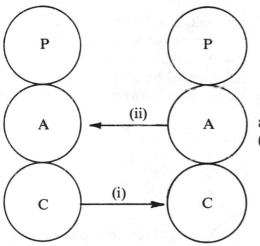

(i) "Let's steal those apples."
(ii) "We may get caught."

Indirect Transactions

This is a transaction in which a third party, usually a child, is brought in, to whom the person is ostensibly speaking, but with the intention of being heard by the second party. It almost invariably ends up as a crossed transaction through the third party, causing unhappiness in all three.

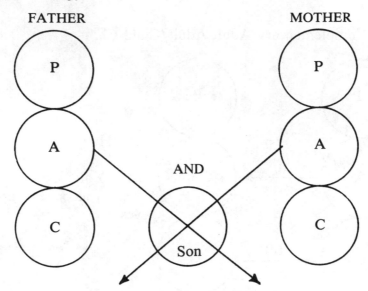

FATHER   MOTHER

AND

Son

Dad (in hearing of Mom): "Do you know how long your mother is going to be, son?"
Son: "I don't know, Dad."
Mom: "I don't know why he is in such a hurry."
Son: "I guess he's anxious to get there before dark, Mom."
This is going to end up as a crossed transaction between the father and mother through the son and it could be obviated by a simple Adult-Adult complementary transaction between the father and the mother, such as:

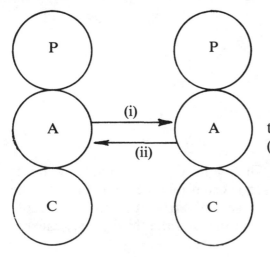

(i) "How long are you going to be, Dear?"
(ii) "About five minutes."

Dual Transactions

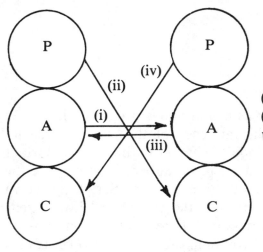

(i) "Where have you *hidden*
(ii) the shoe polish?"
(iii) "In the kitchen drawer
where it always is. (iv)

In this case the Parent components come out in the words "hidden" implying that the shoe polish is not always left in the same place; and "where it always is" implying that the other person never looks in the right place for anything. These end up as crossed transactions. Any number of double, or triple transactions can be employed, but unless the implied meanings of the secondary transactions are either pleasant or humorous, the ultimate result may be a crossed transaction, a cross in the Child and a trading stamp stored for future use. Be careful with multiple transactions!

Gallow's Transactions

This was first described by Claude Steiner (26) and I feel there are more of them and they do more damage than we would imagine. They involve any smiling or laughing reaction to a person's accident or irresponsible behavior. This serves as a Gallow's transaction and tends to reinforce failure.

1. If I smile at my son taking risks.
2. If a teacher smiles at a pupil's stupid behavior.
3. If a mother laughs at a child's clumsiness.

5
Scripting

Berne describes a script as a continuous program, developed in early childhood under the influence of the child's authority figures which directs that person's behavior in the most important areas of his life. It is called a script because it is rather like the script of a play which is given to an actor. The Script lays down quite detailed instructions as to how the person will live. It tells him whether he will be a success or failure in life, in business, in love, in handling finances, in communicating with people. It tells him whom he will need to fill the other roles in his script. It is programmed into the Parent ego state and is acted out by the Child ego state. Each person is forced by his script to repeat over and over the same behavior patterns no matter how much his reason (Adult) tells him that he shouldn't.

It is vital for me to examine myself and the way in which I am living my life to see if I am living it according to the dictates of my Adult or whether I am following a script of life handed down to me by others.

Scripts are passed on from generation to generation through one or more of a number of channels. Families often have a history of a doctor, lawyer or politician in the family and this may lead the youngster to feel that he should emulate his forebears. Is sex sinful or fun? Is childbirth associated with suffering or death? These and other sexual attitudes may influence your script.

Some parents give their children names often associated with the opposite sex or made-up names which may cause the child great embarrassment.

There are many ways in which a child can obtain his script of life and Berne wrote a complete book on scripting entitled *What*

Do We Say After We Say Hello, in which he likened common life scripts to common fairy tales. Although I agree wholeheartedly with the concept of the script and how we can be programmed to play a certain role in life, I feel that to say most people have a "Little Red Riding Hood" script or a "Cinderella" script, is about as dogmatic and prejudiced as Freud's contention that everybody had either an Oedipus or Electra complex. Let us, by all means, be aware of scripting, its dangers and how to escape them, but let us not apply too rigid a classification or interpret them along too preconceived a line. There are many roles which are imparted to the growing Child ego state and indeed, role identification is an important part of the maturation of the healthy person, but the number and variety of life scripts which can be handed down are almost as large and varied as the persons involved.

However, there are a number of factors which should be borne in mind with regard to the scripting of those who look to us for a role in life:

1. Not O.K. children are produced by not O.K. adults.

2. Children are very aware of their not O.K. position.

3. Children would dearly love to feel significant in the eyes of their parents, brothers and sisters.

4. Children are afraid to risk the possibility of rejection and, therefore, put on an appearance of hostility.

5. Mature adults should and must risk themselves repeatedly. From their more reassured position they are in a much stronger position to face possible rejection without suffering the awful feelings which rejection produce in a child.

6. We must again and again establish their significance in our eyes.

7. We must be consistent. Rules must be laid down and then adhered to. It is much better, if possible, to reward compliance with the rules than to punish failure.

8. Adults fulfilling their roles as parents must protect the Parent and Child ego states of their own children from the well meaning but often disastrous effects of the dogma and prejudice of the children's grandparents, even if this does involve a fight with our own parents from time to time. Some of our parents, in their ignorance and with the best of intentions, did a hell of a job bring-

ing us up, but let them not perpetuate this state of affairs in *our* children!

9. Parent tapes which we give our children must come from our Adult ego state.

Our children will then have a lot of good, solid, factual material in their Parent ego state instead of a lot of doubtful material which is going to dominate or influence them to their detriment for the rest of their lives. **We must perform our Parent function with our Adult ego state.** If I perform my parent function with my Parent ego state, I can and may produce a NOT O. K. Child in my grandson, whom I may never meet. When you realize that in the process of maturation, each of us has examined his Parent tapes, taken into the Adult those portions which are reasonable and thrown out those tapes which are unreasonable, then the Parent ego state must be full of unreasonable tapes. Therefore, when we perform our parent function with our Parent ego state we are playing back garbage which our children will record in their Parent as true and receive with their Child with extra repression or rebellion.

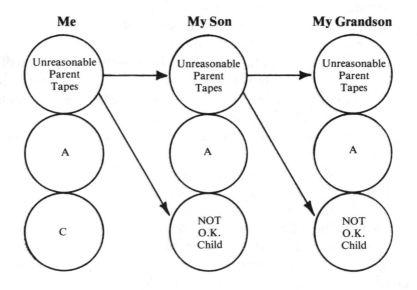

Fig. 5-1 Performing parent function with Parent Ego State

If, however, I perform my parent function with my Adult ego state, a totally different result is achieved:

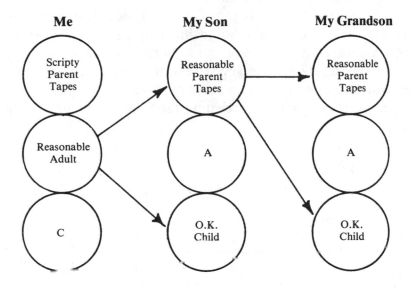

Fig. 5-2 Performing parent function with Adult Ego State

My son will record reasonable tapes in his Parent, so that, even if he does use his Parent on my Grandson, I have, in effect, produced an O.K. Grandson. By this means I have destroyed the tyranny of the past and broken the line along which unreasonable scripts are handed down from generation to generation.

Before leaving the topics of structural and transactional analysis I would like to make a few comments with regard to adolescence and marriage. The adolescent finds it difficult to make adult decisions and, therefore, his Child comes on strongly due to his drive for pleasure and gratification. He sees himself as a grown up but feels himself as a child. The parent must destroy old Parent-Child concepts and replace them with Adult-Adult transactions with the realization that they are very uncertain of themselves and will not risk being hurt, whereas the parent can and must risk it. Teach your adolescents Transactional Analysis. It is an easy concept and they realize that they have something in common with their parents. They realize the role of a parent is not an easy one, that their parents sometimes are acting in their Parent or their Child ego states when they shouldn't be.

With regard to marriage it is a good idea if, *before you are married* you construct a relationship diagram to see how many complementary transactions you normally have with your proposed mate. There are seven sets of complementary transactions which are possible and a score of seven out of seven would be perfect. Most people get married on the basis of one or two out of seven.

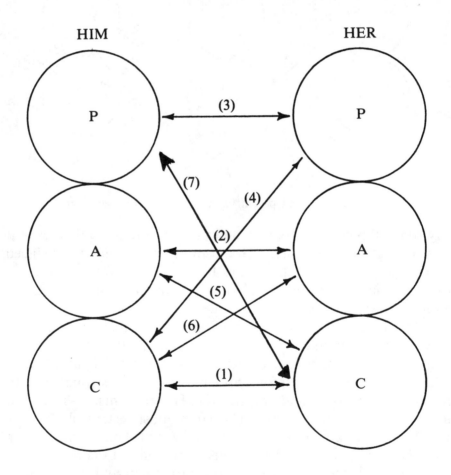

Fig. 5-3 Boy-Girl Relationship Diagram

(1) *Child-Child*

Sex, fun, mischief, feelings, needs, drives.

(2) *Adult-Adult*

Do we have the same interests? Do we have the same friends? Do I like you? Could I stand to face you across the kitchen table for 40 years?

(3) *Parent-Parent*

Do we have the same prejudices and dogmas? Do we have the same culture, religion? Do we have similar views on sex, child raising, sharing of duties, etc?

(4) *Her Parent-His Child*

Is she nurturing to him and does he appreciate it?

(5) *His Adult-Her Child*

Is he a good provider and fixer, and does she appreciate it?

(6) *Her Adult-His Child*

Is she a good housekeeper and mother and does he appreciate it?

(7) *His Parent-Her Child*

Is he nurturing towards her if she is ill?

I feel that if a relationship diagram such as this were to be examined by every couple contemplating marriage, many of the disastrous marriages which we see around us today could be avoided.

What about those marriages which have lost their bloom and are teetering on the brink of destruction? Those in which the partners are silently "serving their time", waiting for the children to grow up, waiting for some miracle or perhaps some other person to come along (in other words, your typical lousy marriage!)?

They have three options:

1. Cut it off cleanly by divorce.

2. Suffer it out until death do us part.

3. Try to make it work by using a combination of Transactional Analysis and the "As-If" principle.

The As-If Principle

Have you ever watched, entranced, while Sir Lawrence Olivier, Kathryn Hepburn, Alec Guinness or any of the really great character actors and actresses become transformed into totally different personalities? They were not just pretending but actually became those people. Act as if you are, and you will become.

Probably eighty percent of those who go into Hypnosis first act as if they are "hypnotized" and then, if they are sufficiently aware of the subtleness of the state, as we shall see in chapter eight, they will notice the altered perception which is characteristic of hypnosis. Act as if you are and you will become.

We have been instructed since childhood to "act bravely", "act calmly", "act wisely". Now I am going to suggest another area in which acting may produce positive results.

I had been seeing a young couple who had been married four years and had two young children. The husband, who had been born and raised in the small town in which they lived, had continued "going out with the boys" after they were married. This involved more and more drinking, more and more quarrels, ending in a black eye, and finally the decision, made by the wife, that it just had to stop.

She came to me and, on hearing her story, I felt that probably the best thing was for them to separate. However, when I saw him and heard his story, I realized that, due to his upbringing in a broken home with a drunken father, he really had not had much of a chance. His life script had been programmed into him very thoroughly and he was acting it out because he was not aware that he did not have to.

We went through the basics of Transactional Analysis and after several sessions they reported a marked improvement in their relationship. They missed seeing me for a couple of weeks over Christmas and the New Year and when they returned they did not look very cheerful and the session started something like this:

Therapist: "How have you been since I last saw you?"

They (together): "Not too bad."

Therapist: "That sounded, to me, as if it was not too good either! What happened?"

Wife (Margaret): "Nothing really."

Therapist: "Did Joe behave himself with regard to drinking during the festivities?"

Margaret: "Oh yes, he did not drink at all and he was quite good with me and the children."

Therapist: "Well, what is making you seem so gloomy?"

Joe (interjecting): "But, how long does this have to go on?"

Therapist: "What do you mean, Joe?"

Joe: "How long do I have to wait and "be good" before I get any sign of affection in return?"

Therapist: "Are you not showing any affection at all, Margaret?"

Margaret: "I can't yet."

Therapist: "Do you want the marriage to get back on track again?"

Margaret: "Yes, but I cannot show any affection yet."

Therapist: "How long are you going to make him suffer for what he has done to you?"

Margaret: "I don't know."

Therapist: "I feel that you are at an impasse, a deadend. Both of you have got to give if you are going to make your marriage work. The bloom has gone off the marriage and it will not return until there is some real affection between you, yet you seem determined not to show affection until the bloom has returned. Result — stalemate. Joe has not been drinking for six weeks and he has been good to you and the children. The dog-house is a draughty place. What if you were to act as if you had more and more affection for him? It would, at least, show effort on your part as well as his."

Margaret: "I could not pretend to show affection. It would be dishonest."

Therapist: "Not if he knew you were acting in order to bring about the change."

Margaret (brightening visibly): "No, I suppose not."

Therapist: "How about acting as if you had just met and fallen in love and try to out-do Sir Lawrence Olivier and Kathryn Hepburn?"

Joe: "How do we start?"

Therapist: "I suggest taking the rest of the day to do something that you both really enjoy, and perhaps cap it with a little sex tonight."

Joe: (showing real interest): "That sounds like a good idea."

Margaret (smiling broadly), makes no comment.

I can only guarantee that this approach will work if two conditions are fulfilled:

1. You must really want it to.

2. You must do what any great performer will do: you must set aside a certain period (say half an hour) in every day during which you rehearse your part as the happily married husband or wife.

Act as if you are and you will become.

6
How
do I Begin
to Cope?

I would like at this point to repeat and summarize my interpretation of the life positions of Tom Harris. Either I can feel O.K.
about myself or I can feel NOT O.K. about myself. Either I can
feel O.K. about you or I can feel NOT O.K. about you. This means
that there are four possible combinations.

I'm NOT O.K. — You're O.K.

This is the natural position of every child. He is totally dependent upon his mother who is almost invariably nurturing during the
first year of his life. If, however, he grows up without changing this
position, he will grow into a *"NOT O.K. Adult"*. He will tend to
put himself down, allow other people to put him down; or he will
internalize his "Not O.K." feelings which will show as physical,
mental, emotional or behavior disorders.

I'm NOT O.K. — You're NOT O.K.

Due to the fact that in early life this person could not rely
upon anyone, he will tend to grow up as *The Hopeless Adult*. He
will tend to gravitate towards the psychiatrist and a long association will commence, during which he will not allow the psychiatrist to help him because the psychiatrist is one of the "Not
O.K." people. He will tend not to get better; and, as Carl Rogers
shows (later) the outcome may well be that the psychiatrist will
deteriorate.

I"m O.K. — You're NOT O.K.

The battered child begins to feel that he is O.K. but nobody
else is. He will tend to grow up as a criminal. He will not allow peo-

ple to help him and, as a consequence, the prison guard tends to become brutalized.

I'm O.K. — You're O.K.

This is the healthy position. Harris goes on to say it is an adopted position. I agree. He has to get rid of his NOT O.K. position. He also says it is a fixed position. I disagree. I believe that we all fluctuate through these positions, but that we have a predominant one.

Having arrived at the understanding that the healthy attitude to life is that of "I'm O.K. — You're O.K.", this still left me with a feeling of dissatisfaction. So! How do I become O.K.? I then did an immense amount of reading and many books later, I came across the work of Stanley Coopersmith entitled *The Antecedents of Self-Esteem*. This is an examination of the many facts and conditions which were prerequisites for the development of self-esteem, or in Transactional Terms "I'm O.K." feelings. He named four major factors:

(i) Significance
(ii) Competence
(iii) Virtue
(iv) Power

Significance

How significant do I feel in the eyes of others? Put in simpler terms but ones which are more difficult to face squarely, I asked myself the question "How many people *really care* for me?". I do not mean how many people have a superficial liking for me, or how many "friends" or how many relatives I have. No, I mean the strictly limited number of people who would really care if I died right now; who would risk their lives for me; who would risk their livelihood for me? When I first asked myself these questions, I developed a nasty feeling in the pit of my stomach when I realized there were very few. My colleagues would doubtless say "Poor old Brian. What a pity for him to die so young." My employees would be out of a job and besides, it would be somewhat messy if I were to drop dead in the office. How many people would risk their lives for me? When faced with that question my "friends" became almost non-existent. "How many people would risk their livelihood for me?" was a question that thinned the ranks even further.

When I came to consider the attitudes of my brothers and sisters, I realized that they would probably be upset to quite a degree, but it would not touch them very deeply, unless perhaps they would feel a sense of personal loss to themselves in that their own circle of significant people had decreased. It would also mean that, being nearly the youngest of the family, this would bring death a little closer to themselves. At the time when I began to examine this aspect of my relationship with others, I was horrified to find how few people really cared for me.

I considered my wife and at that time I could not really be sure. After all, I was fairly well insured and she was young enough to go where she wanted and to do what she wanted. Thank goodness, through mutual effort, this position has now changed, and I can definitely add her to my significant list. At that time my oldest son was thinking a lot about himself and I could not be absolutely sure about him. Once again, with the passage of time and since we had the important transaction mentioned previously, we have become much more close and I have been able to add his name to my list.

With some relief I was able to put on my list the names of my two youngest children, Alice and David. They really care for me, unconditionally, and without ulterior motive.

After some thought I was able to add the name of an aunt, the wife of my mother's youngest brother, who really made me feel significant, and I could also add the names of three men who had been with me in the British Army in World War II. With these I had kept in constant contact through the years and I felt that they would risk a great deal for me.

It was a somewhat sobering thought that at first I could only put six names on my list of significant people and that now, at the age of fifty, I could only put on this list ten people who really cared for me. And yet I felt reasonably adjusted and secure, so perhaps ten is enough. Then I began to wonder how I would feel if I could not put a single name on my list. I could well imagine that at that stage I might consider blowing my brains out. I then asked myself, "What if just one of my children was on my list and nobody else?" In that case I would certainly not commit suicide. This means that if only *one* person in the whole world really cares for me, this makes the difference between life and death. With ten people I am reasonably well off, with twenty I would be wealthy. If anyone tells me they have more than twenty names on their list, I would doubt either their honesty or their judgment.

These somber meditations led me to the following two conclusions: First, most people go through life, bending over backwards, walking on eggs, and endeavoring not to upset the many hundreds of people who don't give a damn for them; and in the process they get knots in their gut which they then go and take out on those very few people who are significant in their lives; those who really care for them. Second, I cannot afford to "put down" any of my significant people, because a "put down" is usually irreversible. If my wife, or one of my children does something stupid (as we all do at times) and I say, "That was a bloody stupid thing to do", I can never retract that statement and they will need me "like a hole in the head". They will therefore certainly not go out of their way to make me feel significant.

At about this time I asked myself a second question: "How many people do *I really care for*?" When it came down to the hard facts, there were not many that I would risk my life for, and perhaps even fewer for whom I would risk my medical licence. So, once again, I sat down to make a list, and to my amazement, I found that I had the same names on both lists. It then became clear to me that if I could make another person feel significant in my eyes, I would automatically become an important source of his feelings of well-being and I would become significant in his eyes. This means that my feelings of significance are one hundred percent within my own control. All I have to do is make another person feel significant.

From this point on I decided that I would no longer try to be "a nice guy" to people who were not significant people. I would not go out of my way to antagonize people, I would always look at people with a view to making them feel significant in my eyes and thus to increasing my significance in the eyes of others, but I would never keep angry or hostile feelings within me when dealing with non-significant people. The list of people who really care for me is too small and too valuable to risk the possibility that I may vent my feelings on them in such a way as to hurt them. This does not mean that I should not express my feelings to those who are close to me, for indeed I should, but I should be careful to express those feelings in reasonable, Adult terms so that I do not "put them down" or decrease their own self-esteem.

A short while ago I realized that I had been putting my son, David, down a great deal. He tends to take a long time to get to the point and if my wife or someone else spoke to me I often used to break off my conversation with David and thus make him feel "I just don't count". I realized what I was doing, so I had a little talk with David and told him that I realized what I was doing and was sorry for it. I told him that if he felt that he had been interrupted again, he was to shout at the top of his voice, "I have been interrupted".

A few weeks later, when we had some guests, David came to talk to me. As usual, he was taking a round about way of getting to the point and my guest interrupted him. I turned back to my guest. Immediately David shouted "I have been interrupted", and stood there looking scarlet. I immediately congratulated him and thanked him for reminding me. We settled his problem and he went away satisfied. I then turned back to my guest and I thought to myself, "Well, if you don't understand, I am not going to try to explain it to you". If he did not understand that was tough. I must not put my own son down because of a guest who was so insignificant that to this day I cannot remember who he was! I have since tried on a number of occasions to remember who that guest was but I simply cannot. In other words, I was going to put down one of the few people who really cared for me for a person whom I cannot even remember today. How many times do we do this to our children? How many times do we make them feel "I'm no good.", "I don't count.", "Nobody wants to listen to me.". No wonder there are so many "Not O.K." adults!

Competence

Competence can be expressed as a ratio of results over aims. If I set out to be a member of the Toronto Maple Leafs hockey team and I only make it into the local hockey team, this would be

like a ratio of one to ten, and I would feel incompetent. If my aim
was to get into the local team and I made it, I would have achieved
that aim and I would feel competent. This can be expressed in
another way:

$$\text{Competence} = \frac{\text{Work hard enough}}{\text{Set realistic goals}}$$

We have to set goals for ourselves. The human being is like a
bicycle, If it isn't going somewhere it falls over, but these goals
must not be too high. They must be goals which we know we can
attain. If I set out to be President of the Canadian Medical
Association I would end up as an embittered old man. For one
thing I am not in medical politics. I am on no committees, and
therefore, have no experience and am not well known; and there
are only possibly another ten to fifteen presidents to be elected
before I retire. If I set this as my aim, I am going to feel incompetent. If, however, I set as my aim that of being a reasonably competent general practitioner with a special interest in the psychosomatic disorders, then I might make it. With regard to working hard enough, one should not try to spring clean the house in
one day. A little at a time, but done well, is what is important. If I
remember this basic concept, then I have one hundred percent control over my feelings of competence.

Virtue

The next condition which Coopersmith considered of importance was virtue. He defines this as adherence to a code of
religious, moral or ethical values. This word makes me think of going to church on Sundays, or contributing more money than my
neighbor to a particular charity and, to me, is associated with
hypocrisy. It also denotes standards of conduct set by others.

Therefore, I would like to substitute *Integrity* for the word
virtue. It implies wholeness, uprightness and honesty and is more
consistent with maintaining self-imposed standards of conduct,
rather than other-imposed values. Feelings of Integrity would,
therefore, satisfy the needs of the Adapted Child on the basis of
standards imposed by his own Adult after examination by Reason.

Power

The fourth condition mentioned by Coopersmith was that of power. How well can I influence others? I would imagine that Billy Graham would have feelings of power in that he can sway a congregation; Howard Hughes would have had feelings of power in that he could buy people; if my son were out with a group of his buddies and they said to him, "Let's go and drink this bottle of rye in the car", and he said, "No, let's go and play basketball instead", and they went to play basketball, then he would have feelings of power. If, however, they said, "To hell with you", and went to drink their bottle of whiskey in the car and he joined them, he would have a loss of feeling of power. Personally, I feel that if one has power or the ability to influence other people this would enhance one's feeling of self-esteem. If, on the other hand, I try to influence other people and fail, I should not allow myself to be put down by it. I have known many people with absolutely no power but great self-esteem because they had feelings of significance in the eyes of others and competence in themselves.

Another objection which I have to the use of the word Power is that it is often associated with corruption. I, therefore, feel that, in the same way that Virtue, as used by Coopersmith, is better replaced by Integrity, it would be more meaningful to replace the word Power by Assertiveness.

If I am non-assertive and I allow other people to "put me down", to walk all over me, to push ahead of me, then my self-esteem will suffer. However, if I am sufficiently assertive that I do not allow these things to occur, then my self-esteem should be good even if I have absolutely no power.

I could imagine that there are some hippies on a downtown mall in any town who feel significant in the eyes of their buddies, who feel competent at playing their guitar, but who have absolutely no power. However, their self-esteem is good and you had better not try to walk all over them because they are quite assertive!

Coping with Guilt

To Coopersmith's four conditions for self-esteem, I feel it is necessary to add a fifth: Coping with Guilt. Guilt is a very real thing with which we all have to contend. In our examination of our guilt feelings we have to decide first of all whether the feeling is based upon truth or falsehood. If it is false — if it is based on some prejudiced Parent tape, such as, "Boys don't cry.", or, "Nice girls don't wear lipstick", then it should be thrown out ruthlessly. If the guilt feelings are based upon truth you have to decide whether this is something which is present or past. If you have guilt feelings over something which is past and cannot be rectified, then you have to learn to live with it and cope with it and not allow it to interfere with your life now. If I did something in World War II and was guilty but not caught, then I have to learn to live with it. No amount of self-recrimination will take it away. I must accept myself as I am, with my past, and learn to live in the present. If you are doing something presently which makes you feel guilty, then the easiest thing is to stop doing it.

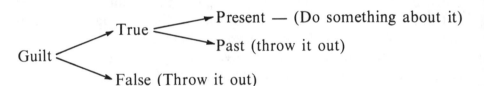

I believe it is most important if we can substantiate the theories of one authority with those of another. The first two conditions for the establishment of self-esteem as expressed by Coopersmith, that is, Significance and Competence, tie in very nicely with the needs of the Child as expressed by Berne and Harris, namely,

1. Stimulation
2. Recognition
3. Structure

Recognition may be by others. If I am recognized by others, I am going to feel significance in their eyes. Or, I may give myself recognition for something which I have done and shall feel competence in my own eyes. I can structure my time with rituals and pastimes, which are trivial, or games and withdrawal, which are destructive; or I can fill it with activities, which will give me feelings of competence; and with intimacy, which will give me feelings of significance.

Hans Selye says that we should work in order to be able to take pride in excellence (which will make us feel competent). His jingle: "Fight for your highest attainable aim, but never put up resistance in vain", is expressing, in more poetic terms, the ratio of

$$\frac{\text{Results}}{\text{Aims}} = \text{Competence}$$

Hans Selye also says the gratitude of others is the only commodity which I can hoard, and which nobody can take away from me. This is saying, in other words, that I must become significant in the eyes of others. To do this I must make them feel significant in my eyes and I must be competent in what I do for them. Therefore, the Altruistic Egotism of Hans Selye equals the Significance and Competence of Coopersmith, which satisfy the needs of the Child as defined by Berne and Harris.

Integrity, adherence to a reasonable standard of honesty and law, is necessary to enable the Free Child to become sufficiently adapted to live in an ordered society. Integrity therefore satisfies the needs of the Adapted Child.

Assertiveness, a learned skill, which enables me to express my feelings adequately without being aggressive or defensive, and prevents me from being manipulated or exploited, helps me to deal with my repressions.

Coping with Guilt, a rational process, initiated and maintained by the Adult, is necessary to dampen down, even if it does not completely eliminate, feelings of guilt.

This integration of the theories of Coopersmith with those of Berne and Selye not only substantiates all three, but gives me a definite plan to follow in order to feel O.K. about myself:

I must feel significant in the eyes of someone else, and to do this I must make him, or her, feel significant in my eyes.

I must make my wife feel significant in my eyes today. (Have I done so?) I must make my children feel significant in my eyes today. (Have I done so?) Tomorrow or next Thursday is too late! (I suggest you put this book down, now, and do or say something to make them feel significant in your eyes.)

I must feel competent in my own eyes. I must set reasonable goals: immediate, intermediate, and long-term. If I don't, I shall drift.

I must set and adhere to standards of integrity which will not make me feel guilty tomorrow or next year.

I must be quietly and firmly assertive and not allow unexpressed feelings to accumulate.

I must rationalize my guilts, reject false guilts representing pre-judiced Parent tapes, put behind me those true guilts which are past and rectify those which are present.

This represents a daily check-list for me to follow. This is not just an interesting theory but a practical tool for me to use.

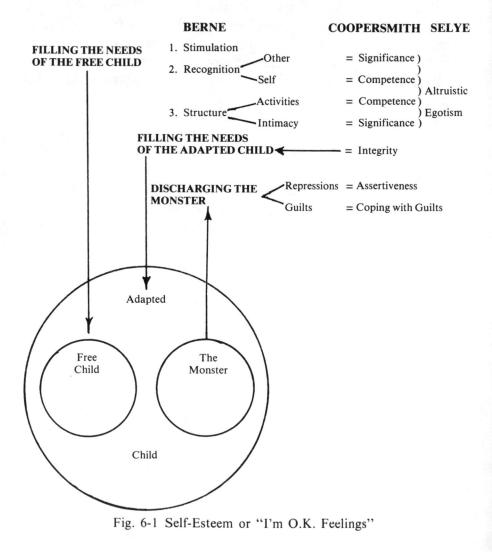

Fig. 6-1 Self-Esteem or "I'm O.K. Feelings"

7

Relating to Others. Is This Important?

Carl Rogers was one of the pioneers of Interactional Psychology, believing that psychological health was due mainly to healthy communication between people. He believed that therapy should be non-directive, that the patient should be allowed and encouraged to express all his feelings and that the therapist should not give advice nor comment on those feelings. He should limit himself to reflecting in his words what the patient felt so that the patient would know that he was being correctly and completely understood.

He was very much of a free-thinker and was prepared to defy accepted theories and to come to conclusions based upon his own observations: "Neither the Bible nor the prophets; neither Freud nor research; neither the revelations of God nor man can take precedence over my own direct experience". (*On Becoming a Person*, p. 24).

Tempering this attitude was his belief that if you did not expose yourself to criticism, then you were unlikely to make any progressive discoveries either.

Carl Rogers did not regard a human personality as being something static, to be measured, altered or cured. He considered it to be in a constant process of change. A person never "arrived", but was always in the process of "becoming".

He believed that man had a basic drive towards positive accomplishment, towards growth, towards maturity, towards self actualization. He was one of the first of the new school of psychologists like Abraham Maslow and Eric Berne, who tended away from the concepts of life being predetermined and irrevocably fixed by one's early conditioning or the mystical complexes inspired by tortuous imaginations. He felt most strongly that, in working with and attempting to understand other human beings, one could always find a strong impulse towards positive growth.

During his many years of psychotherapy, Carl Rogers found that the "therapy" as such, really did not matter! Therapists of such divergent schools as Psycho-analysis, Behaviorism, Gestalt, Transactional Analysis, or Reality Therapy could be equally successful with their patients provided certain conditions were established in the relationship between the therapist and the patient. If the conditions were established, the patient would almost certainly get better. If they were not established, the patient may well become worse! Therefore, the understanding and establishment of these conditions for successful psychotherapy becomes of paramount importance. Carl Rogers' critera were: self-acceptance, congruence, empathy, and positive unconditional regard.

Self-Acceptance

In his many years of experience he began to formulate a concept which I shall paraphrase, "The curious paradox is that when I can accept myself **as I am** then I change; and when I can accept you **as you are** then you change". Rogers found that the more he was able to accept both himself and the patient as they were, then the more change seemed to occur in both of them. Therapy became a mutual growth process.

This does not mean that I must *like* everything about myself. It does mean that I must accept myself as a person with gross imperfections, because if I cannot accept myself, as I am, then I do not have a starting point from which change may occur. Also, if I cannot accept myself, as I am, then how can I hope to accept anyone else?

This first criterion of Rogers always struck me as being very strange in that it seemed to be the very opposite of the affirmation of all the "positive thinkers". The positive thinkers all stated, in effect, "Decide what you want to be, tell yourself that is what you are; and that is what you will become".

It was only after thinking about it a great deal that I realized I had experienced a number of occasions myself in which the fact that I had been able to accept another person as he or she was had enabled them to change.

The first episode occurred over twenty-five years ago, before I had even decided to study medicine. I was working as a clerk in an office in Toronto. There was another young, single man in the office, and all the rest of the staff were older and married. We therefore tended to chum around together, go for a beer together, or go swimming in Lake Ontario.

One summer day he suggested we go for a hike up the Don Valley. We had been walking for some time when he suddenly said, "Brian, do you know why I asked you to come up here today?", to which I replied that I did not. He then went on to tell me that he had a sex problem, and so I said, "Join the club. I don't get enough myself", or something to that effect. He then replied, "No, mine is much worse than that. I can only achieve sexual satisfaction if I excrete on the girl's breasts." I looked at him and said, "You've got a problem! I honestly don't know what you should do about it but I strongly suggest that you go and see somebody who has more experience in this sort of line, such as a psychiatrist, because, quite honestly, it is outside my experience."

We then carried on walking and neither of us mentioned it any more. We had a couple of beers and went our respective ways. When I met him again on Monday morning in the office my immediate reaction was, "Well, he's still my buddy and as long as he doesn't try to shit on my chest I don't really care." So, we continued to chum around together and neither of us mentioned it again until about three months later when he suddenly said to me, "Brian, do you remember me telling you about myself a few months ago?" I said, "Yes, did you see anyone about it?" And he replied, "No, it hasn't bothered me since and I have been out with several girls and had quite normal and satisfying relations with them." I said, "Great", and I didn't think about it again until about twenty years later.

Then I began to study Rogers' work and I wondered if

perhaps that was an example of my acceptance of him *as he was*, enabling him to accept himself *as he was* and thus to change.

Another more recent occasion, occurred in the course of seeing a pleasant, middle-aged lady, with several children. She had been referred by a doctor from another area. She was apparently happily married and they had no financial or other worries. It did not seem, on the surface, that there could be any circumstances causing her symptoms.

She appeared in my office about every six months over a course of about two years. Each time she came it was with an almost overwhelming fear that she was going to take a knife and cut her wrists. We would sit and discuss her fears for one or two sessions, after which she would disappear for another six months and then the cycle would start all over again.

On the last occasion she visited me, she came into the office, sat down, and burst out with, "I should have told you this two years ago, Doctor, but I didn't because I thought you would not want to see me again. Anyway, I have decided to tell you everything".

Haltingly, she then told me her story. Some twenty years before, she had been in prison on a drug offence. She had shared a cell with a woman who had been convicted of manslaughter but she knew that, in actual fact, it had been murder. The woman actually bragged about it. This woman was big, strong and aggressive, and made my patient do all her chores for her and tried to humiliate her in every conceivable way.

Finally, feeling that she must get back at her tormentor in some way, and yet fearing to show open rebellion, my patient, when ordered to make cocoa for her cell-mate, had stuck her finger up her rectum and smeared it around the inside of the mug before making the cocoa. This gave her great satisfaction at the time, but about five years later, after marrying and starting a family, she began to have terrible guilt feelings which led to her being in my office.

My immediate reaction to her story was to laugh and to say that I thought it was a very clever way of getting her own back under the circumstances and I doubted if I would have been so clever. I felt that the whole situation in which she found herself had been so dehumanizing that I did not consider her reaction to the brutality of this woman as anything but normal. We continued chatting for awhile, during which she seemed to want to laugh a lot, and then she left.

The next day she phoned me and said that when she had left my office, the day before, she felt as if she was walking about two feet off the ground. While she was driving home she had thought to herself, "Dr. Gorman did not recoil in horror when I told him about myself, in fact he laughed, and he doesn't even love me; so, why the hell can't I tell my husband?" She then told me that she had told her husband the previous night; a thing which she had never dared to do during all the fifteen years of her marriage. I asked her what her husband's reaction had been and she replied, "He laughed just like you did".

From time to time since then this lady has telephoned me to say that she has had no more problems with suicidal thoughts; that she feels a much closer relationship with her husband; and that she is very grateful that I had encouraged her to expose herself to me. I have not seen this lady since but there have been no recurrences of these suicidal thoughts for over six years. So, it would seem to be true that when I can accept you as you are, then you can accept yourself as you are, which enables you to change.

For this reason, if a woman comes to me and says, "My husband is an alcoholic. Will you treat him?" I will say, "No." If, however, the husband comes and says, "I am an alcoholic. Will you treat me?" I will say, "Yes." However much other workers stress the importance of congruence, accurate empathy, and non-possessive warmth, I feel that Rogers' criteria of Self-Acceptance and Other Acceptance rank every bit as high.

Congruence

If I were to walk into a home and tell a person that his father had just been killed and while saying it I had a smile on my face, my expression of feelings would be said to be incongruent. Congruence is the opposite of this. It means that my apparent expression of feelings is in line with what I am saying. What I say must ring true. There must be no false fronts. The patient must know exactly where he stands with me. Sidney Jourard has written at great length on the subject of transparency. I must be transparent with my patients if I expect them to be transparent with me. He must see me as I am, another human being with weaknesses which I accept even if I don't like them. If I pose as the great doctor who is going to make some grand analysis of his squalid problems, then I am doomed to failure. I sometimes leave a therapy session with the feeling that the patient has learned a lot more about me than I have about him, but this seems to be balanced sooner or later, and very often sooner by much greater revelations by the patient than I would normally have expected.

I was dealing at one time with a middle-aged man who was sorely troubled by something, but I could not put my finger on it. We got to reminiscing about experiences in the army in World War II and I admitted to being involved in circumstances which were extremely discreditable to myself, if not downright criminal. I did not know at the time why I felt it necessary to make these revelations. To my amazement, within five minutes, the patient told me that what was bothering him was that he had embezzled a large sum of money from his firm. Since then the firm had changed hands, and the auditors had inspected the books and had not found the fraud. He desperately wanted to give the money back but could not give it back to the rightful owners. I am certain that I would not have learned this story if I had not been transparent about myself.

Empathy

To have empathy with a patient, I must be able to express in *my* words what *he* feels to *his* complete satisfaction. I must be able to express what he is feeling in such a way that he may say, "Yes, you've hit the nail right on the head", or, "I couldn't have described it better myself".

At first I tend to fall down on the establishment of Empathy; and the reason is that I talk too much and do not listen enough! Well, I do this deliberately because Carl Rogers would take up to 80 hours to establish empathy. I believe that most of my patients are intelligent people and that many doctors tend to underestimate their intelligence and talk down to them or not at all. I strongly believe that, if I define my terms and build a theoretical framework of personality into which they can fit themselves, I am likely to achieve results much more quickly than if I merely listen to their problems and paraphrase them.

I have also found that, if I am sufficiently transparent while discussing my theories, the patient may identify with some of the things I disclose and reach a level of self-understanding sufficient to solve his own problems before I have achieved accurate enpathy — and this, after all, is the object of therapy. Therefore, where Rogers laid more emphasis on empathy, I feel that the congruence, transparency and self-disclosure of the therapist are the more important factors.

Positive Unconditional Regard

In order to be effective, I must like the patient, regardless of his behavior, condition, mood or opinions. I must be non-judgmental. I cannot say what he should have done or ought not to have done. There must be absolutely no conditions or strings attached to my regard for him. This may seem to be an almost impossible condition to fulfill and in some cases it is, but if a therapist has difficulty in this area with more than a few patients, then he should not be in psychotherapy.

CLIENT-CENTERED THERAPY

With the establishment of these four criteria in the relationship as a means whereby change is going to be made easier, Carl Rogers then developed a method of approaching therapy called "Client-Centered Therapy" in which the client or patient was permitted complete freedom from any form of directiveness on the part of the therapist. He would discuss what the patient wanted to discuss and would limit his own participation to paraphrasing or repeating in his own words what the patient had said. As therapy progressed, the patient would come to understand that he was being understood; that he was being accepted as he was; that he could express his true feelings without the threat of judgment by the therapist.

Truax and Carkhuff (28) in their book *Towards Effective Counselling and Psychotherapy* compiled an impressive evaluation of Rogers' work and made some further interesting observations:

1. The average results of psychotherapy were statistically shown to be ineffective. The fact that a large number of therapists were shown to get good results with their patients indicate that a large number must get bad results; or be what they called "psychotoxic".

2. They stressed in particular what they describe as the therapeutic triad of accurate empathy, non-possessive warmth and genuineness, but they do not stress the self-acceptance and other acceptance upon which Rogers laid so much emphasis.

3. They reaffirmed the well-established fact in counselling theory that attitudes are changed very little by advice, persuasion or threats.

4. They noted that certain characteristics in the therapist should be avoided:

a) Anxiety or defensiveness

b) Clinical detachment.

The patient must be aware that the therapist is sure of himself and that they are not a "case" to be studied. The whole of Truax and Carkhuff's book was a scholarly-presented mass of data designed to test and prove their theories and to my mind, they presented substantial and impressive results.

My own experience with the works of Rogers, Truax and Carkhuff, is that their criteria cannot really be improved upon. However, I think that certain changes in emphasis have, in my own experience, been warranted and in fact, necessary:

a. I agree wholeheartedly with Rogers' Self-Acceptance and Other Acceptance. I stress again that I do not have to like all the things I see in myself, or in my patient, but I do have to accept them.

b. I believe the positive unconditional regard has indeed to be positive and unconditional and I feel that the "non-possessive warmth" of Truax and Carkhuff, while it may be safer for the emotional stability of the therapist, would tend to lead to the adoption of the very "clinical detachment" which they warn against. Rogers points out repeatedly the therapist must feel sufficiently strong within himself not to be overwhelmed by the patient's response to his unconditional positive regard or love. I believe "non-possessive warmth" is not warm enough and I like to consider this condition for successful psychotherapy to be "positive unconditional regard which is non-possessive".

While agreeing with these conditions as being a necessary matrix upon which the therapy is woven, I find the method of Client-Centered Therapy, while doubtless effective, is unnecessarily time-consuming. Most of the patients whom I see have no knowledge of psychology, the factors which influence the formation of personality, the factors which cause the growing personality to deviate from the path most likely to lead to self-fulfillment, or the conditions likely to facilitate such growth. They know nothing of the conditions in the relationship which are required, nor the conditions which are conducive to the development of self-esteem. Therefore, I have deliberately deviated from their method in the initial sessions. I feel that if I can explain to the patient a reasonable theory of personality, how it develops, what factors can cause it to deviate, how these factors can be modified or dealt with, and what conditions are most likely to produce a positive change, then many hours of therapy can be eliminated. If I give the patient credit for the often high order of intelligence which he possesses, and explain to him what I am trying to achieve, as well as giving us a common language with which to reach accurate empathy, the therapy can be both effective and brief.

The conclusion at which Rogers arrived after his many years of research and which has struck me as most important, was his concept that therapy was not a "one way street"; that if the patient improved, then the therapist improved; that as the fulfillment of the four conditions of self-acceptance, congruence, empathy, and positive unconditional regard came about, there was a strong movement towards growth in both the patient and therapist. This has immensely wide implications. It means that if any two people can establish these four conditions in their relationship, they are both going to achieve greater fulfillment of their potential. It means that if I can establish these conditions with a patient and he can, in turn, establish them with his wife, I will have, in effect, treated his wife without ever having met her. But to do this, he must understand what I am trying to do and why.

I would like to relate one case history in which a patient was referred to me by another doctor with severe asthma which was obviously of psychological origin. However, the patient refused to see me. He said, "I have asthma. I don't need to see a Shrink." A few days later this patient's wife came to see me and said, "How are we going to get my husband to come and see you?" I replied, "You can't." Then she said, "Well, what do you do? What is your treatment about? How does it work?" So I began to tell her something of what I did. After a little while she said, "I think I'll sign up with you for a few sessions for myself", and so I agreed. It soon became apparent their marriage was not as good as they would have liked, but after about three or four sessions she said that she was feeling much better. I then said it was a pity I had not seen her husband because he was the man I had been asked to see. She replied, "In no way are you going to see my husband. Since coming to see you I have learned how to deal with my husband and I am not going to let you upset the applecart by treating him." I laughed and said, "Well, I suppose there's nothing I can do about it."

Some three months later she rang me and said, "Doctor, I thought you might be interested in this. Last night I went with my husband to his firm's Christmas party and as we got in the door, his boss came over to me and said, "I have noticed an enormous change in George in the last few weeks. About two months ago I was thinking of letting him go. His work was so poor, he was having attacks of asthma, and he was not getting along well with the other members of the staff. However, during the last few weeks there has been this remarkable change. His work has improved and he is now the best man I have." This lady realized that her husband had been improving during the period when she had herself been seeing me for treatment. This does seem to lead me to believe that if these four conditions can be established between any two people both will improve and it is not outside the bounds of possibility that the patient had been treated, as it were, by remote control.

Another important conclusion which I reached from the study of Rogers' criteria, was that if I can accept myself as I am and accept you as you are; if I am congruent, genuine, sincere; if I can understand you as completely as it is possible for one person to understand another; and if I can love you regardless of that understanding, then I am practicing the essence of the spirit of Christianity without any religion or churches or dogma or rules. A couple of years ago I was giving a talk to a church group on Transactional Analysis. All the group had read *I'm O.K. — You're O.K.* by Dr. Harris and we were discussing the four life positions. At the time, although I could accept the statement that the "I'm O.K. — You're O.K." position was the healthy position, I had difficulty within myself in reconciling it with the statement that it was also the Christian position. It was only several sessions later when the discussion had become sidetracked onto Rogers' criteria and I was writing these conditions in block letters on the chalk board, that suddenly it hit me that, in actual fact, Rogers and Harris had arrived at the same point. Although starting from different positions, having different backgrounds, different training, different experience and using different terminology, they had both defined the healthy attitude to life which was also a good Christian (Moslem or Hindu) mode of living. If I put a bracket between Self-Acceptance and Congruence; if I accept myself as I am and if I am genuine and sincere, then, "I'm O.K."

If I put a second bracket between Empathy and Positive Unconditional Regard; if I can understand you so well that I can express in my words what you feel to your complete satisfaction; and I love you regardless of that understanding, then, "You're O.K."

I can remember to this day the feeling of elation, of awe and of gratitude that I had suddenly been able to see the total integration of their concepts of the attitudes necessary for health. Not only that: Rogers' criteria told me a lot more about how to become O.K. myself. I must accept myself *as I am*. I must accept you *as you are*. I must be genuine and sincere. If I put on a "front" people may like the "front" but it is not me. If I let people know me truly, perhaps they may dislike what they see — but they may also like me and I have added to my Significant People. I must try to understand other people so well that I can express in my words what they feel to their complete satisfaction. If I can really do that, I will find it difficult to argue with them or dislike them.

I felt something like Archimedes must have felt when he got

into his bath and the level of water rose in the tub by the exact amount of the volume of his body and he thus discovered how to measure the volume of irregular solids. I wanted to jump out of the bath and streak to the king shouting "Eureka"! It was, I feel, what Abraham Maslow would have considered a "peak experience".

I feel there are two more important points, which came out of Rogers' work, which should be emphasized. One is that psychotherapy is a two way street. If the patient gets better, the therapist gets better. If the patient gets worse, the therapist gets worse. It is an established fact that the incidence of suicide, marital disruption and nervous breakdown is extremely high among psychiatrists. Therefore, I feel that everyone doing psychotherapy should evaluate the standard of his own work to determine whether or not he is placing his own sanity in jeopardy. I am prepared to lay my own sanity on the line for any new patient for up to ten hours. At this point I will carefully evaluate the situation. If there is no progress I will terminate therapy either by referring the patient elsewhere or changing the mode of therapy to that of tranquillizers, anti-depressants, etc. If there is progress, but it is slow, and I do not feel myself personally threatened, then I will continue treating the patient, but only on a session-by-session basis.

The second important implication which stems from the work of Rogers is that everybody is either a psychotherapist or is actually destructive in their relationships with other people. If I can establish in my relationship with any other person, the four conditions which are necessary for mutual growth, *then we will both become better.* If I deliberately do anything to hinder the establishment of these conditions, then we are both likely to get worse.

This means that we all bear a great responsibility not only for our own mental health, but also for that of others. If I can set up growth conditions in my relationship with six people and these, in their turn, can establish the same conditions with six more people, then I have directly touched the lives of thirty-six people. The implications are staggering.

CARL ROGERS' CRITERIA		TOM HARRIS' LIFE POSITIONS
1. SELF ACCEPTANCE If I can accept myself **as I am** **2. CONGRUENCE** and am genuine and sincere	))))))))	Then : I'm O.K.
	AND	
3. EMPATHY If I can understand you so well that I can express in **my** words what **you** feel **4. POSITIVE UNCONDITIONAL** **REGARD** and like you regardless of that understanding	)))))))))))	Then : You're O.K.

Fig. 7-1 Integration of the Theories of Rogers and Harris

8
Relaxation

I have deliberately used the word relaxation because the word "hypnosis" has always held for me connotations of power, magic, mysticism and the occult. I feel these are commonly held beliefs and because of this, hypnosis has not attained its proper status as one of the modes of treatment that can be highly successful for a limited range of problems. Hypnosis is also a useful method of changing the self-image in the direction of growth leading to "self-actualization".

Because of this, when I feel that hypnosis may be beneficial, I devote an entire hour to an explanation of it (as far as I am able) and to exploding and debunking the myths, prejudices and gross misinformation with which some people approach this subject.

I have found over a number of years, that the best approach is to explain to the patient my own doubts, fears, prejudices and hostilities on the subject and how I have gradually overcome each, and now accept it as a useful therapeutic tool with extraordinary advantages in some cases and definite limitations in others. It is not the "be all and end all" of psychotherapy, but a useful adjunct to be woven in with the other approaches of attitude and behavior modification to form a comprehensive method. I start my explanation with the concept that the human mind could be likened to an iceberg floating in water with only one-tenth of its mass above the surface. Diagramatically I illustrate it as a three-sided pyramid with one point above the surface and three points below.

The conscious mind is represented by one point which indicates that the conscious mind is only capable of thinking of one thing at a time. The sub-conscious mind has many functions which

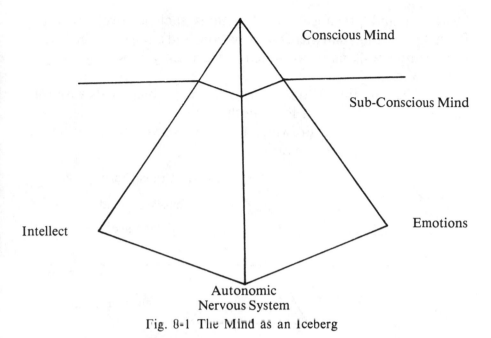

Fig. 8-1 The Mind as an Iceberg

are all acting simultaneously and can be, to oversimplify it, divided into three main areas:

1. The Intellectual Area dealing with memory, thought processes, etc. Wilder Penfield (19) in his classical experiments, found that if certain areas of the brain are stimulated by electrodes, a memory can be recalled in far greater detail than one can normally remember voluntarily, and this is also accompanied by the feelings associated with this particular memory.

2. The Autonomic Nervous System. This, together with its closely related accomplice, the hormone gland system, controls all the bodily functions which fall outside the sphere of the conscious mind, such as the control of breathing, heart rate, blood pressure, blood chemistry, body temperature, and a host of other conditions. Some of these are controlled by the conscious mind and subsequently, relegated to the sub-conscious; and some of these are controlled mainly by the sub-conscious mind but their control can and often is taken over by the conscious mind. Examples of these are learned techniques which require considerable conscious concentration during the learning process but which are relegated to the sub-conscious when sufficient proficiency is obtained. Others are

hysterical and psychosomatic functions such as over-breathing, flushing, fainting, diarrhea, constipation, and a host of other symptom complexes, many of which we are only now beginning to understand.

3. The Emotional Area. This is the part which deals with such emotions as fear, anger, love, faith, etc.

Now, for ease of drawing, I would like you to examine one side of our three-sided pyramid.

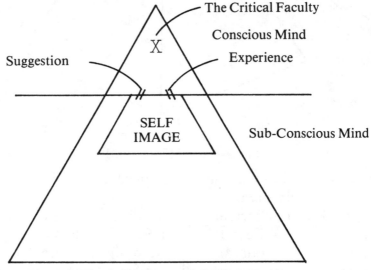

Fig. 8-2 The Self-Image and Critical Faculty

Within the sub-conscious mind, and a part of it, is a picture of ourselves which we will call the Self-Image. This has been in the process of formation since birth. It has been developed through two doors, experience and suggestion. (Everything which we experience about ourselves from birth is recorded and it is recorded as the infant sees it, without criticism and without editing.) In fact it is swallowed whole (or introjected as the Gestaltists would define it). It may be true or it may be false, but as far as that infant is concerned it is true because he has as yet no means of testing it against reality. He, therefore, builds a self-image or picture of himself which is true as far as he is concerned and he proceeds to act his life as if it were true — in fact, he has no alternative. If he was clumsy as all children are, and he was repeatedly told that he was stupid and clumsy, then both experiences and suggestions would tend to validate and confirm his stupidity and clumsiness and he would continue to act in a manner which was consistent with this self-image.

It was at this stage in my thinking that I began to read all the books I could lay my hands on dealing with "positive thinking"; and all of them said, in effect, that if you can change your self-image by positive thinking, then you can change yourself. All I have to do is to decide what I want to be; tell myself that is what I am, and that is what I will become. This sounded wonderful to me and I thought that all I had to do was give myself some good "positive suggestions" for a few weeks and I would be a superman. Unfortunately, months later I had the same "hang-ups" as before.

Suddenly it struck me the positive thinkers were leaving out one very important fact which, to my mind, seemed crucial. In the conscious mind, and growing with it, parallel to the self-image of the sub-conscious mind, was a function which I shall call the *Critical Faculty*, which was constantly scrutinizing all new suggestions and experiences which were not consistent with those concepts which I had already accepted as true and rejecting all such inconsistent data.

If I were to tell my eighteen-month-old son that the blotter on my desk was blue (when in actual fact it was green) he would accept it because "Daddy said so"; whereas if I told him the same thing when he was ten years old, he would reject it because his experience would tell him that it was the same color as the plant on my desk.

Therefore, I decided that in order to feed new constructive suggestions and experiences into a person's Self-Image, I must find ways of suppressing or circumventing the Critical Faculty of the conscious mind. I could think of three ways in which this could be done (there may be more, but I can only think of three):

Strong emotion

a. **Fear.** If I was in a field with a four-foot fence around it, I would not even consider the possibility of jumping it at my age. If, however, an angry bull was charging me, the strong emotion of fear would suppress my Critical Faculty and I would clear the fence with six inches to spare. This suppression of my Critical Faculty would have released powers which transcended those of my Self-Image.

Another example of fear suppressing the Critical Faculty was given in an article in the Edmonton Journal in 1970. This story was about a lady weighing 110 pounds, who was driving a little English car weighing 1100 pounds, and she had her seven-year-old son in the car. She skidded off the road and rolled the car. Her son was thrown out and trapped underneath the car but she was unhurt. She looked around in desperation for help but there was nobody in sight. So, she lifted approximately 550 pounds and got the boy out. At that time, two men came along in a car and saw what she had done and rushed over to help her but, by the time they had got there, she had already freed the boy. They were so amazed that the two of them tried to lift the side of the car which they had *seen* her lift and they could not even move it. The strong emotion of fear had suppressed her Critical Faculty and given her access to powers which she didn't even know she had.

b. **Mass hysteria and religious or racial prejudice.** One has only to look at the Third Reich in Germany or Northern Ireland today to see how these strong emotions can and do suppress the Critical Faculty and cause ordinary people to perform actions which are not rational.

c. **Faith.** If you happen to be a Catholic you may go to Lourdes, if a Moslem to Mecca, if a Hindu you may dip yourself in the river Ganges, and if your faith is strong enough some rather remarkable things can occur. George Bernard Shaw, the author, made the observation that at Lourdes he had seen many hundreds of pairs of crutches and many wheel chairs which had been left behind by people who no longer needed them, but that he hadn't seen a single case of a wooden leg or a glass eye. This meant that the miracles did not extend to replacing limbs or organs but allowed people to use joints and muscles which they hadn't used for a long time. This does not exclude the possibility of miracles, but it does indicate the enormous powers of faith.

Sleep

The second circumstance under which the Critical Faculty of the conscious mind can be suppressed is during sleep. When I am asleep my conscious mind is inactive and with it the Critical Faculty. However, the sub-conscious mind is constantly aware of what is going on around. For example, for thirteen years I was responsible for a small country hospital and the telephone bell never rings twice in my house at night. My wife does not hear the telephone and I can be called out four times and she won't even know about it. However, if one of the children were to vomit, my wife would be awake instantly, and I would not stir. If there is a noise downstairs we will both wake up because this could be a fire or a burglar. In other words, we are listening for those things which we want to hear, which are important to us.

When we are asleep the sub-conscious mind is listening for, and will accept, any suggestions which it wants to hear. I first used this when my little girl broke her leg. After setting it in a cast I brought her home. Later, when she was sleeping, she was very restless and in obvious discomfort. I went into her room and said, "Alice, you will soon find that the pain has gone from your leg, you can turn over quite easily and will be able to sleep peacefully for the rest of the night." Instantly, the creases in her face disappeared, and she turned over and slept soundly. I have since used sleep suggestion on all my children with some remarkable results with regard to their abilities at school and their feelings of security and self-reliance.

I began to wonder how I could use this in my practice but decided that if I started creeping into people's bedrooms to give them suggestions I might get shot, or suffer a fate worse than death. I tried making little cassette tapes but found that these were not very satisfactory in that the patient tended to wake up when the tape came on. It was also time-consuming, as far as I was concerned, because I had to go to the clinic in the evenings to make an individual tape for each patient.

Hypnosis

It was at this time that I stumbled across a third means of partially suppressing the Critical Faculty of the conscious mind and this was hypnosis. I would like to be able to give you a concise, scientific definition of hypnosis but I cannot because none yet exists which explains all the phenomena of this condition. There have been many definitions of hypnosis which have been considered valid for a time, only to be replaced by another, but none at this moment precisely defines it.

In my explanation to patients (which I consider the most important part of the hypno-therapeutic technique) I use, basically, three definitions, all of which are to a greater or lesser degree true, and yet none of which is completely true.

The first definition which I consider to have some merit is *A state of super relaxation in which suggestions, for your own good, are accepted with reduced criticism.* This is quite a good definition but it is not complete. It lacks something. I was explaining this to a patient of mine about a year ago and he said, "Yes, I'll agree with that because I went up onto the stage for a professional hypnotist about two years ago. The hypnotist told me that I was in the Sahara Desert. I knew I was on stage and I knew the audience was down there, but I felt so hot that I had to take my tie off, and I could feel the sand in my shoes. Then the hypnotist told us that he was going to give us each a glass of absolute alcohol and we were going to become very drunk. Well, there was no way that I was going to do that because I am a Mormon, so I just sat there while all the other people on the stage drank the imaginary alcohol and behaved as if they were drunk." He was not asleep; he was aware of where he was; he would not do anything which was against his principles; but it is hard to explain the sand in his shoes.

The second definition of hypnosis is *A form of role-playing or acting* in which the subject acts as if he were hypnotized. In a paper, "A Preface to the Theory of Hypnosis" by Robert W. White (30), he says, "Hypnotic behavior is meaningful, goal-directed striving, its most general goal being to behave like a hypnotized person as this is continuously defined by the operator and understood by the subject. The subject knows what is going on, infers the intentions and hopes of the operator, and he does his best to oblige. Even when we urge him beforehand to resist us or afterwards coax him to remember what we have ordered him to forget, he decides as best he can what we really want and he strives to give it to us."

At one stage in my investigations of hypnosis I made a point of going to a number of theatrical displays. I went around afterwards and spoke to the people who had been up on the stage as subjects. I would say to them, "Excuse me, would you mind telling me how you felt when you were on the stage?" I was somewhat surprised to get, almost invariably, the same answer, "Well, I really didn't think I was hypnotized, but as everybody else seemed to be, I thought I had better go along". The next person I asked would reply, "I didn't want to spoil the show and everybody else was hypnotized so I thought I would play along." It seemed as if everyone thought that they were the only person who was not hypnotized and yet, to the audience it seemed as if they all were. So I began to think that hypnosis was just role playing in which the act of playing the role of the hypnotized person, in some way, conferred upon the subject the characteristics of the state of hypnosis. This is not completely true either because I have, many times, used hypnosis very successfully on children for bed wetting or behavior disorders who have no knowledge of hypnosis and cannot, therefore, be role playing.

The third definition which I use in my explanation to patients is that hypnosis may be a form of *conditioned response* in which the patient is given suggestions which are, at first, completely acceptable; but that these suggestions become less and less acceptable until they become, frankly, unacceptable.

For example, the therapist holds his thumb about four inches away from the patient's nose and tells the patient to look at his thumb. He then says, "As you look at my thumb your eyes will become very tired." This is a very true statement and the patient naturally accepts it because the thumb is being held too close to his eyes. The therapist then says, "And as your eyes become more and more tired your eyelids will become heavier and heavier." This is also true, because your eyes are being strained and therefore, your eyelids are becoming heavy, and so you accept this also. The next suggestion is, "And as I bring my thumb towards the bridge of your nose your eyes will close and you will drop into a deep state of relaxation." This suggestion is not as acceptable as the first two, but you accept it anyway because by this time your eyes are tired and you have accepted the two previous suggestions, so you close your eyes.

The therapist may then suggest you imagine yourself going down an escalator while he counts slowly from one to ten. Or he may ask you to imagine yourself lying on the beach of a tropical island, feeling the hot rays of the sun penetrating your skin and the soft, warm sand under your body while you listen to the sound of the waves breaking on the shore. He may then say something like this: "Now I want you to put your two hands together with the fingers interlocked and I want you to squeeze your two hands very tightly together; so tightly that they feel as if they are stuck together." You can quite easily imagine this and you are imagining your hands to be tightly stuck together when the therapist suddenly says, "So tightly stuck together that you cannot pull them apart however hard you try." Here you come to a contradiction. *If you want* to go into hypnosis, *you want* your hands to be stuck together, and as you have accepted all his preceding suggestions, you tend to suppress the Critical thought that you could, if you wished, pull your hands apart quite easily. You, therefore, accept his suggestion and go deeper into hypnosis.

There are some merits to this theory also, but it cannot be entirely true because some people use techniques which do not require words to be spoken, such as in the Direct Stare technique, or Erickson's (5) Surprise Arm Levitation Technique. When you put these three apparently unrelated definitions of hypnosis together, you begin to realize it is a very complex state indeed.

It was at this stage in my studies that I decided to take a formal course in hypnosis at Banff. When I received the prospectus for the course it stated that the wives of the participating doctors were cordially invited into the seminar *free*. My wife's immediate reaction was that she was not going to be used as a guinea-pig for anybody! I replied that she did not have to do anything she did not want to do, but suggested that she should come for the social part of the course. "O.K.", she said, "but no monkey business!" While we were driving towards Banff I started to have misgivings myself. I was not sure that I wanted anybody "monkeying with my mind" either. I still, despite my readings on the subject, felt that I might be putting myself in someone else's "power". I was, therefore, an extremely critical observer during the introductory sessions.

The guest lecturer had with him several trained hypnotic subjects, who needed only to be touched on the bridge of the nose with the hypnotist's thumb to go into a deep "trance". This looked very impressive. He would go up and down the line putting people into hypnosis and bringing them out again and I began to think, "My goodness, this man has a powerful thumb". He then showed us that even with well trained subjects he could not make them go into hypnosis if they did not want to. He then proceeded to go down the row touching each person on the bridge of the nose with his thumb and they sat there and laughed at him. This was a very impressive point as far as I was concerned. We continued watching the demonstrations with keen attention and I was able to elicit certain facts:

Facts Learned by Observation

1. *You only go into hypnosis if you want to.* Nobody can make you go.

2. *You only go as deeply into hypnosis as you want to and can.* I noticed that when he was going down the row putting people into hypnosis, sometimes a person would go deeply and sometimes shallowly. The hypnotist could not make any person go deeper than they wished to go. He may say to one man, "Bill, you don't seem to be very deep this time. Would you like to go deeper? If you would, just raise your index finger." Bill would then raise his right index finger and the hypnotist would give him suggestions to help him to go deeper; but he could not make him go any deeper than he wanted to go.

3. The third factor, which I learned by observation, was that the hypnotist may go down the row of subjects putting them into hypnosis and by the time he got to number six, number one could be sitting up and looking to see how the other five were getting along. *This means that you can come out of hypnosis any time you want to.* My wife and I discussed these three factors and decided that if you only go into hypnosis if you want to; if you only

go as deeply as you want to, and if you can come out any time you want to, then hypnosis must be safe and nobody can "monkey with your mind". If a hypnotist tells you to do or say anything you do not like, you can open your eyes and tell him to go to hell.

We decided, therefore, that we must experience this ourselves. I went to the chief instructor and asked if he would hypnotize me. "Sure", he said, "Sit down and concentrate on my thumb", which he held about four inches in front of my nose. "Now, your eyes will quickly become tired; your eyelids will become more and more heavy; and as I touch you on the bridge of the nose with my thumb, you will close your eyes and drop into a deep state of the most profound relaxation." He then told me to imagine myself in a series of relaxing situations like going down an escalator and lying on the beach in Hawaii. He did not even challenge me by telling me to interlock my hands and squeeze them tightly together. He just told me to open my eyes, which I did. "Well, how do you feel?" he said. "O.K." I replied, "but I don't think I was hypnotized." "Why not?" he said. "Because I was wide awake and acutely aware of my surroundings, the noise in the hall around us, and the fact that I could get up and walk away any time I wanted to." "So you could", he replied, "but you didn't." He then went on to ask me to answer two questions:

Was I more relaxed than I usually am? And to this I replied, "Yes, slightly."

Was I accepting his suggestions with reduced criticism? To this I replied that I was, because I wanted to learn and because I thought he was a nice fellow and I did not want to disappoint him. He then said that it did not matter what my motive was but that if I was more relaxed than normal and if I was accepting his suggestions with reduced criticism, I was satisfying the criteria for the first definition of hypnosis and I was in hypnosis by definition whether I felt it or not. I felt this was not valid because hypnosis has not been scientifically defined. I was grossly disappointed.

My wife then tried and her reactions were similar to mine. She did not think that she had been hypnotized either. At this point we almost decided to go skiing. Here we were, in Banff, in February. We had paid for the course. It was going to cost us money for hotel rooms and I was going to lose three days' earnings, so the course was going to be quite expensive and we felt that we were wasting our time, so we might just as well convert it into a skiing trip. However, there was about an hour before lunch so we went back into the hall to see what they were up to. Both of us felt that hypnosis was a washout. One of my friends then asked me if he could practice on me. I replied that I was a very poor subject but that he could if he wished. He replied, "I want to practice my technique, so just *pretend* for me please." So, I pretended I was going into hypnosis. I began to realize that, with this complete novice, practicing for the very first time, I was somewhat more relaxed than I had been with the internationally known expert. I thought this strange, so I asked another doctor to practice on me and I pretended again. The third time I became even more relaxed than the second time.

So I *pretended* with three more doctors in quick succession and by the time I had done this six times I was aware of the fact that I was achieving a most profound state of relaxation, amounting almost to an altered state of consciousness. I suddenly realized that I did not need them; that I was learning to go into hypnosis and that I was getting better at it with practice and that this did not depend upon the skill of the operator.

Facts Learned by Experience

1. *You are not asleep.* You are acutely aware of your surroundings. I had been expecting to be in some sort of "trance", "state", "coma", and to be stretched across between two chairs and have someone sit on me.

2. The second factor elicited by experience is that *it is a learned skill which improves with practice and does not depend upon the skill of the operator.*

3. The third fact I learned by experience was that, as I practiced, I seemed to go deeper and become more relaxed, so that by the time I had tried it six times I was aware of a very deep state of relaxation. I was aware of an altered state of consciousness. I was also aware of the fact that I had been in hypnosis the first time with the internationally known expert, but because I had been expecting *too much* I had missed it. Because of these expectations, I had missed the rather subtle thing which is hypnosis. *Therefore, the*

third fact which I learned by experience was that you must not expect too much. If you expect to be in a trance, or state, or coma you will miss it. If you expect to be relaxed, then you will achieve it. It is, I think, very unfortunate that the word "sleep" keeps cropping up in techniques of hypnotic induction, because it gives a totally incorrect impression. I have explained this concept of not expecting too much to a number of people who have used marijuana or hashish and when I have done so their eyes have filled with the light of understanding. Several of them have told me that the first time they smoked it, they wondered where the "trip" was and why everyone else was "stoned" but not them. It was only after smoking it several times that they found that the trip was a learned experience which was somewhat subtle. I am therefore putting in this explanation to enable those who have used "pot" or "hash" to understand hypnosis more fully. It is a learned skill, a state of mind, a self-induced "high".

I realized at that point I had almost missed hypnosis because it had not been adequately explained to me. If I was going to use hypnosis in my practice, I must pay particular attention to the explanation which I give to my patients. I returned from Banff and started using hypnosis. I would spend an hour explaining hypnosis, more or less as I have done here, and then I would say to the patient, "Would you like to try it?" If they said, "Yes" I would go and get the appointment book and make an appointment for them to come back later. Most of the patients who returned went into hypnosis immediately but some didn't and I could not understand it. I thought that, with the sort of explanation which I had given to them, everybody should be able to go into hypnosis.

It was only in the September of 1970 that I realized what I was doing wrong. If I spend an hour explaining hypnosis to a patient and then ask them if they would like to try it, I am putting pressure on them to say "Yes". If I then get the appointment book and make the appointment for them myself I am compounding that pressure; some patients must have been saying "Yes" but meaning "No", and you only go into hypnosis if you want to!

I, therefore, made a rule, in September 1970, that I would explain hypnosis to the patient, to the best of my ability, and then I would tell him not to make a decision here and now; but would ask him to go home and think about it for a few days. Then, after mature consideration, if he decided he wanted to try it, he had to make the gesture of ringing the clinic and making the appointment specifically for a first session of hypnosis. He had to tell my receptionist to put under his name, in red ink, the word "yes". Then, when I looked at the appointment book for the day, I would know that this particular patient was coming back, of his own free will, with the expectation of going into hypnosis and that I had not put any pressure on him at all. I knew that the next time he walked into my office he was already in hypnosis and all I had to do was to show him how to go a bit deeper.

During the eight years since I made this rule I have had sometimes as many as eight new patients a week for hypnosis, sometimes as few as two. If we take the smaller number, two patients a week for eight years is over 800 patients and since I made that rule, everybody who has come back for hypnosis, after the explanation, has gone into hypnosis the first time and been aware of it (and I can only think of about half a dozen who have not returned after the initial explanation). This is not to say that I have cured all the patients that I have seen since then, for indeed I have not, but at least they have learned to achieve a degree of relaxation which they were unable to obtain before.

During the introductory session I try also to dispose of two misconceptions which occur as the result of the patients having witnessed stage hypnosis. The first is that the hypnotist seems to have such *power* over the subject. I explain this by saying that every stage hypnotist knows that if he has an audience of 100 people, there are at least twenty people in that audience who are highly suggestible. He, therefore, tells the audience to interlock the fingers of their hands and place them on the top of their heads and to stare into his eyes. He then stands in the spotlight, in total silence, looking very impressive, for about two minutes. Suddenly he will say, "Your hands are stuck together. You cannot pull them apart however how hard you try. Try!" About eighty out of the hundred will pull them apart and laugh, but about twenty will believe that their hands are stuck together. If you believe that your hands are stuck together you will not try hard enough to get them apart!

The hypnotist has, therefore, already selected the good subjects. He will then ask them to come up on the stage so that he can release them. This is the most critical part of his performance because, while they are coming up onto the stage, he has to make an individual character assessment of each subject. He must pick those people who *want* to act on the stage. The first person may come onto the stage with a big smile on his face as if to say, "Look, aren't I clever. I'm hypnotized!" The hypnotist recognizes that this person is a born performer and so he snaps his fingers and tells him to take his hands down and sit on a chair on the stage, because he wants him. The next subject may come up onto the stage with an expression on his face as if to say, "I hope none of my neighbors are in the audience." The hypnotist will know that this person would not perform for him on the stage and so he snaps his fingers, tells him to take his hands down and go back to the audience.

The hypnotist will end up with four or five subjects on the stage who are not only good subjects but who *want* to perform on the stage. Therefore, if he asks them to row a boat in the ocean, they will row *because they want to*. If he tells them there is a mouse running across the stage, they will climb up on their chairs and scream. He may make a mistake in assessing a person's character and this person will sit in the chair and will not do anything he is told. The attendants quickly get rid of this man because he is spoiling the show. He may offer a Mormon a drink and he won't drink it, but occasionally he will get an exceptionally good subject, and most hypnotists learn to recognize these very quickly, and this person can be stretched between two chairs and have people sit on him.

Now, everybody believes that this is due to the power of the hypnotist but there is no more power being shown by the subject stretched between two chairs than there was by the lady who lifted the car. The hypnotist, therefore, has knowledge and he has skill but he has no power. All he is doing is utilizing the sub-conscious power of the subject, and the subject is loaning him that power for the purposes of the demonstration and can take it away any time he wishes.

The second misconception is related to reports which have been made in the newspapers in which a person has been hypnotized on the stage and has gone home and has "gone back into hypnosis", and the hypnotist has had to be called to "bring the patient out". When you realize that you only go into hypnosis if you want to; you only go as deeply as you want to; you can come out any time you want to; you are not asleep; and it is a learned skill which improves with practice; then you realize that you are not dealing with hypnosis in this case but with hysteria.

If a hysterical subject is in the audience and he believes the hypnotist has power over him, he can go home and have an attack of hysteria and become paralyzed, or anesthetic, or any other form of hysteria. This is to my mind the only danger of theatrical hypnosis. If the patient or subject is aware that the hypnotist has no power and if they are aware of all the other factors which I have explained, then hypnosis is absolutely safe.

Hypnosis is, therefore, a safe, but curiously indefinable condition; a state which is not a state, a trance which is not a trance; a skill which comes from within but which may be directed either from within or from without; and which is useful for a limited number of conditions, the chief of which being those which are associated with a high degree of emotional stress or tension.

It is a state, moreover, which can be reached by following numerous avenues:

For the very suggestible (20 percent of the population), simple suggestions are all that are required.

For the less suggestible (perhaps 75 percent of the population), role-playing or acting is required to enable them to distract their conscious mind and allow the sub-conscious to do its job. They act hypnotized, they become hypnotized and they acquire some of the characteristics of hypnosis, such as altered perception and the reduction of the critical faculty.

For the remaining 5 percent of the population, who have difficulty in acting, it may be necessary to condition them to reach the same state.

Thus, we can see the three "definitions" which I gave earlier are not, in fact, definitions, but different means of achieving the same state — hypnosis — which still defies definition! It also means that these avenues are no longer conflicting but complementary and that anybody can achieve hypnosis if they understand it and want to.

Hypnosis in transactional terms

During the early development of the Ego, a number of things are happening: the Parent is being bombarded by dogma, prejudice, authority, criticism, inconsistency and thousands of untested bits of information.

The Child is a mass of insecure feelings, unfulfilled needs and instinctual drives. The Adult has, at that time, insufficient information in its computer bank to make valid judgments, not only with regard to the facts of the outside world, but also with regard to the loudly playing Parent tapes and the clamoring urges of the Child for instant gratification.

During this time a great deal of untrue fact and inappropriate feelings get through the poorly programmed Adult reason and become incorporated in the Parent and Child compartments of the Adult as "true" when in actual fact they are not. These "facts" are acted upon as "true" and go into the makeup of the self-image and this limits, controls and frustrates the functioning of the healthy Adult ego state. The Parent and Child compartments of the Adult ego have been "contaminated", and so our thoughts, feelings and actions are contaminated in life. What would appear on the surface as an Adult statement or reaction is often really the result of invalid parental programming, overwhelming and inappropriate Child feelings, harmful or excessive instincts or drives, or grossly unfulfilled needs which have not been recognized or updated by the Reason of the Adult.

Hypnosis in transactional terms I would like to consider as a means of suppressing the Critical Faculty (The Reason of the Adult) and allowing the barriers between the Parent, Adult and Child within the Adult to become permeable or porous, and so to enable updating to take place. In this way, in the relaxed state of hypnosis, Child feelings become less overwhelming and Parent dogmas less threatening. The Reason can update, reevaluate, reject, and reorganize those "facts" which have until that time formed that picture of "self" which has governed my thoughts, feelings and actions with regard both to myself and to my environment.

EXPERIENCES

1) Real
2) Imagined

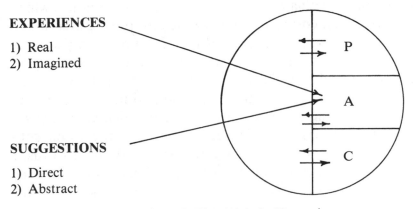

SUGGESTIONS

1) Direct
2) Abstract

Fig. 8-3 The Adult in Hypnosis

During this state of hypnosis, not only are the internal boundaries softened and made more porous, but the Critical Faculty is partially suppressed to allow new experiences and suggestions to go towards the making of a new self-image. The self-image is made up of suggestions which we have received and experiences which we have undergone. In hypnosis, suggestions can be accepted which record over the old imprints. These suggestions may be either direct or abstract. Direct suggestions have to be reasonable and acceptable or the Critical Faculty will "spring to life" and reject them. Abstract suggestions, on the other hand, do not have to be quite so reasonable as no direct suggestion is being made with regard to a specific subject, and, therefore, the Critical Faculty is less likely to reject them.

With regard to experience, this may be either real or imagined. In hypnosis one is able to experience real relaxation and feelings of well-being which will in time replace habitual tensions which have interfered with the individual's ability to function at maximum efficiency. With regard to imagined experience, the sub-conscious mind does not know the difference between a real experience and one which is vividly imagined. The sub-conscious mind is at the mercy of the interpretations, which are made by our brain, of signals received through our sensations of sight, sound, smell, touch and taste.

If I am walking through a tropical forest and I see a snake, the light stimulus travelling from the snake to my eyes will be transformed in the retina of my eyes into a nervous stimulus which goes to my occipital cortex and then to the interpretive area where it is recognized as "snake". Messages then flash out to my adrenal glands and my motor nervous system to enable me to do whatever is necessary to avoid being bitten by the snake. Suppose what I actually saw was a branch of a tree. The light stimulus goes to my eye, the nervous stimulus travels to the brain which *misinterprets* the message as "snake". This sets in motion the same sub-conscious mechanisms as if it were a real snake. In other words, I *imagined* I saw a snake and my sub-conscious cannot tell the difference between a real experience and one which is *vividly imagined*. We can, therefore, use imagined experience in the un-critical state of hypnosis to rebuild our self-image and its responses to the environment in the same way that our self-image was built originally by real experiences.

9
Application
of Hypnosis

Only after a very thorough explanation of hypnosis, what it is, and what is more important, what it is not, does the patient come back for induction. When he comes back, I go over the important points that the patient must remember:

1. You only go into hypnosis if you want to.
2. You only go as deeply as you want to.
3. You can come out any time you want to.
4. You are not asleep — in fact you are as wide awake as you are when you are just sitting in the office talking to me.
5. It is a learned skill which improves with practice and which does not depend upon the skill of the operator.
6. You must not expect too much.

I give the patient a demonstration of hypnosis, using my secretary or my wife. I do this for two reasons.

a. If hypnosis is a form of role playing or acting, then it gives the patient a role to follow. It also lets them know what to expect.

b. It eliminates the last vestiges of fear because they can see that there is absolutely nothing to be frightened of.

The induction I use is a passive relaxation induction, purely by the use of words and without the use of any "gimmicks" such as thumbs for them to stare at or watches on chains.

I use a fairly standard form of induction in which I adopt a very relaxed attitude, either lolling in my chair or partially draped over my desk (a form of non-verbal communication of relaxation). I then say, "I would like you to make yourself comfortable, close your eyes, and take some nice, deep breaths. When you breathe *in* you will feel your chest rising and when you breathe *out* you will feel your chest falling. Now, I want you to concentrate on breathing out. Every time you breathe out I want you to imagine yourself sinking down into the substance of the chair and becoming more and more relaxed and comfortable. And every time you breathe out I want you to let your chest wall collapse just like a balloon being pricked by a pin; and as your chest wall collapses and all the muscles of your chest go loose and slack, I want you to feel this wave of relaxation going through your whole body so that every time you breathe out you will become more and more deeply relaxed and your arms, and legs, and neck will become loose and floppy, just like a "Raggedy-Ann" doll, deeper, and deeper and deeper. More and more relaxed and comfortable."

Pause . . . "Now I would like you to imagine that you are stepping onto the top of a long escalator going *down*. There is no one else around you and you have the whole place to yourself, and as you feel yourself sinking down on the escalator, I want you to feel yourself becoming more and more relaxed and comfortable. While you are sinking down on the escalator, I am going to count for you slowly from 1 through to 10, during which I want you to let yourself become even more deeply relaxed so that by the time I reach the count of 10 you will be at the bottom of the escalator feeling very, very relaxed indeed." I synchronize my counting with the patient's expiration as follows: "One, going down slowly . . . . . two, very, very relaxed . . . . . three, very, very comfortable . . . . . four, deeper and deeper and deeper . . . . . five, half way down the escalator . . . . . six, sinking steadily further and further down . . . . . seven, all the tension going out of your body . . . . . eight, deeper and deeper and deeper . . . . . nine, nearly there . . . . . ten, right down at the bottom of the escalator feeling very, very relaxed indeed."

At this stage, they may have predetermined how deep they will go, and will think they have reached that level at the bottom of the escalator. I therefore then say, "Now I would like you to step off the escalator, walk forward about ten paces and get onto the top of a second escalator which is going to take you *very much* deeper." At this stage it is often easily observed that the patient becomes very much more relaxed. I then follow the same counting sequence, altering the words only slightly for each count. I then ask them to imagine themselves being transported on a magic carpet to a beautiful South Sea island where they are lying on the soft, warm sand, feeling the hot rays of the sun penetrating their skin, and hearing the sound of the waves breaking on the shore. I then continue, "And while you are lying there, beautifully relaxed and comfortable, I want you to concentrate on the muscles of your calves; let them go completely loose, relaxed, and comfortable; and I want you to feel this relaxation spreading up into the muscles of your thighs, then into your abdomen and chest, through to your back, across your shoulders, down your arms, up the muscles of your neck to your face and scalp, everything completely relaxed and comfortable."

I then use one of two methods of deepening the state of relaxation, the first being that of arm levitation. I will say to them, "I am now going to pick up your right hand, and as I raise your right hand you will feel it becoming lighter and lighter so that it is beginning to feel as if it is floating there absolutely without any weight at all." And as I raise the hand I begin to allow my fingers to slip away from the wrist so that they receive a non-verbal message that I am going to let their hand go and that I want them to keep their hand up in the air. By the time I have let go of their wrist, their hand is floating in the air apparently weightless. Then I will say, "Now, the weight is gradually returning to your hand and it is beginning to sink down towards the arm of the chair and as it does so you will feel yourself becoming more and more relaxed and comfortable, so that by the time your hand reaches the arm of the chair you will be very, very deeply relaxed indeed."

It is very often surprising how the patient will keep his hand up in the air for quite a long time and then very, very gradually lower it onto the chair. And by the time his hand reaches the chair he is obviously in a very deep state of relaxation, completely and utterly immobilized, without moving a muscle, very, very deeply relaxed indeed.

The second deepening technique which I sometimes use, but not as often, is: "Now I would like you to put your two hands together with your fingers interlocked and I would like you to squeeze your two hands together very, very tightly . . . . . so tightly together that they *feel* as if they are *stuck* together . . . . . so tightly stuck together that you cannot pull them apart however hard you try. On the count of three your hands will become unstuck and will drop loosely into your lap and you will drop into the most profound state of relaxation . . . . . one . . . . . two . . . . . three." I then start giving suggestions to the patient and while I am doing so I am watching for certain specific signs:

1. I time the patient in their first session of hypnosis and after it is over I ask them to tell me how long they thought they were lying perfectly still. They usually will say two, or four or five minutes, when in actual fact the whole process takes about 17 or 18 minutes. This indicates that the patient has had complete distortion of their sense of time.

2. I watch for the degree of immobility of the subject. If they are achieving a very deep state of relaxation they are completely immobilized for the full 18 minutes — something one does not normally see in a person who is just sitting in a chair.

3. I time their respiratory rate. The normal rate of respiration is about 16 breaths per minute. I find it not uncommon for the respiratory rate to drop to 5 or 6 per minute, even on the first session, and in one or two cases I have had patients who only breathe about twice a minute. This indicates, to me, such a profound degree of relaxation that the metabolic rate has slowed down to the extent that their requirements of oxygen are materially reduced.

Ego Strengthening Techniques

According to the theories of structural and transactional analysis, the original Life Position taken by every child is "I am not O.K. — You're O.K." The way that this is changed into the stance of "I'm O.K. — You're O.K." is by the satisfaction of the needs of the Child for stimulation and recognition, leading to a sense of identity, self-esteem, and "O.K. feelings". Therefore, a fundamental part of my hypnotherapy is to give suggestions for the strengthening of the self-esteem of the patient. I use two types of ego strengthening suggestions, either direct or abstract. Initially I use direct suggestions with everyone, but as I explain the theories underlying the therapy, I can bring more abstract techniques into the manner of giving suggestions.

Direct Ego Strengthening Techniques

The following is an example of the type of direct suggestions which I use, modified, of course, for each particular patient:

"You have become so deeply relaxed that your mind has become very receptive to anything that you *want* to hear. Anything that I tell you in this receptive state will, *if you wish*, make a deep and lasting impression upon your sub-conscious mind; and these impressions will daily exert a stronger and stronger effect upon the way you think, upon the way you feel, upon the way you behave, and upon the way in which you can learn to control all your emotional and bodily functions. Because of this deep relaxation, you will feel healthier and stronger in every way. You will have a greater zest and enthusiasm for life. You will enjoy doing what you have to do. You will experience life as a challenge which will give you great satisfaction.

You will steadily develop greater and greater control of both your nervous system and of your hormone gland system, which between them control all the functions and conditions of the body. In this way, all symptoms and signs of ill health or disease will disappear, and your heart, lungs, stomach, and other organs, glands, muscles, nerves, joints and skin will function with increasing health and efficiency. You will develop great resistance to all forms of infection or allergy, and you will feel physically better and better every day.

Every day your nerves will become stronger and steadier, your mind calm and clear, more composed, more tranquil, more relaxed, more confident. Your memory and concentration will be improved. You will have complete control of all your thoughts and emotions. You will develop a greater feeling of self-esteem, a greater feeling of personal well-being, safety, security and happiness than you have ever felt before.

Every day you will develop more confidence in your own worth and ability. You will become more capable of setting and achieving goals in life which are realistic, worthwhile and progressive.

Every night, you will go to sleep quickly and easily; and you will sleep deeply and refreshingly, and awake in the morning feeling calm, relaxed, confident, and cheerful; and ready to meet all the challenges of the new day with boundless energy and enthusiasm.

Your sub-conscious mind knows your problems. It also knows the solutions to those problems, and it can, and will, either resolve them completely or allow you to adjust to them so that they no longer cause you distress or disease. In this way your body will always function in complete balance and harmony to maintain a state of glorious and abundant physical, mental and emotional health and well-being.

The powers of your sub-conscious mind are almost infinite. Any limits which exist are those which you have placed there by your thoughts about yourself or have been placed there by the suggestions and experiences which have been imposed upon you by others. These limits can be removed by changing those thoughts. Picture yourself exactly as you would like to be in every detail. Pause . . . . . (in here I fit the sort of things which would suit the particular patient concerned). Hold this picture of yourself firmly in your mind at all times. Have faith in the almost infinite power of your own sub-conscious mind to transform you into a living image of that picture. Slowly but surely you will become that which you have clearly and persistently imagined for it is a fact that everything about you, both good and bad, first began as an image in your mind.

Today, you are starting to believe in yourself more than ever before. As of now, you can expect, from your own sub-conscious mind, the ability and power to enable you to do whatever you wish or need to do in order to be healthy, happy, and successful. As you become more and more relaxed through daily practice, and as you develop a proper attitude towards yourself and your life, you will begin to see things in better perspective and begin to set realistic goals. You will realize that *nothing* in life is worth the price of worry; that no people or things should be allowed to dominate you; that no task or situation or circumstance is so important that it should be allowed to interfere with your health or happiness. As you become daily more relaxed, calm and tranquil, you will find all the tension has gone out of your body and that your tendency to (headaches, ulcers, diarrhea, asthma, eczema, etc.) will have gone completely and forever, and that you will feel right with yourself, right with those around you, and right with your environment."

An Abstract Technique of Ego Strengthening

It has long been apparent that a marked difference exists between hypnosis under experimental and therapeutic conditions. In the former, the subject is participating voluntarily and in a detached frame of mind, and the results of the experiment do not intimately and vitally affect him. He can, therefore, sometimes perform actions which transcend those of his voluntary capacity.

Under therapeutic conditions, however, the subject is acutely aware of the fact that the results of therapy may have a most important effect upon his subsequent feelings of well being. His state of mind is, therefore, not detached but, on the contrary, he is both anxious and critical.

The anxiety can usually be allayed by even a light level of hypnosis but the Critical Faculty of the conscious mind would appear to be active even in the deeper states; scrutinizing all suggestions to determine whether or not the suggestions are acceptable.

There are two factors involved in the acceptability of a suggestion. The first is that of *motivation*. Many people have symptoms which they would like to lose, but not if it involves any effort on their part. A person may wish to stop smoking, but his desire to stop is usually not as strong as his desire to satisfy his gratification habit. Hypnosis is only effective when there is a strong desire on the part of the person for it to be effective. A casual wish is not enough.

Under these circumstances, direct suggestions for the removal of the gratification habit will usually fail. However, results can sometimes be achieved if the patient is presented with abstract thoughts with regard to the strengthening of motivation.

The second factor involved in the acceptability of a suggestion is that of *credibility*. If a patient has for many years experienced a phobic reaction under certain circumstances, or has had manifestations of psychosomatic disease, it is not reasonable to expect them to disappear as a result of direct suggestion. The patient will tend to become critical and as his Critical Faculty becomes aroused, the hypnosis will lighten and the suggestions become ineffective.

One means of circumventing this Critical Faculty, which seems to be operative to some degree under all therapeutic situations, is to give suggestions in an indirect or abstract manner, in such a way that no direct suggestion is made, and therefore, the Critical Faculty is less likely to be activated. During the last few years I have found that a modified form of Dr. John Hartland's (11) excellent Ego Strengthening delivered in this abstract manner, has been very effective. The general technique which I have used, altered, of course, to suit each patient, is as follows:

"You are now so deeply relaxed that your mind has become very receptive to anything that you *want* to hear. Anything that I tell you in this receptive state will, *if you wish*, make a deep and lasting impression upon your sub-conscious mind; and these impressions will daily exert a stronger and stronger effect upon the way you think, upon the way you feel, upon the way you behave, and upon the way in which you can learn to control all your emotional and bodily functions.

The powers of your sub-conscious mind are almost infinite. Any limits which exist are those which you have placed there by your thoughts about yourself or have been placed there by the suggestions and experiences which have been imposed on you by others.

These limits to your own powers can be removed and your self-esteem and feelings of worth can be restored by changing your thoughts about yourself and by reaffirming your belief in the power of your Adult ego state always to act in a reasonable manner so that you can no longer be overwhelmed by the inappropriate feelings of your Child nor by the dogma and prejudice of your Parent, to cause either emotional disorder, bodily symptoms, or irresponsible behavior; either towards yourself or others.

Your sub-conscious mind has absolute control of all the functions and conditions of your body. It is like a powerful computer which has been programmed to work constantly towards a state of perfect physical and mental health and it works automatically to produce this state of health unless interfered with by stress.

Because of this deep relaxation which you have achieved; and because of the greater understanding which you have of yourself; and because of the practice which you are beginning to make of always expressing your feelings, assertively, through your Adult Ego State, your sub-conscious mind is being freed from the damaging action of repressed emotion and allowed to perform its natural task of returning you to a state of complete physical and mental health.

Because the critical part of the conscious mind is never completely suppressed; and as I wish you to remain as uncritical as possible, I am going to ask you just to think about certain words and their possible meanings and associations *for you*. I want you to think lazily of these words, to let them float around in your mind, to let them sink deeper and deeper into your sub-conscious mind until they become woven into the very fabric of your substance and your self-image.

The first word 1 would like you to think about is the word "health" and I want you, now and always, to associate it with the word "good". What can the words "good health" mean? They can mean a sense of superb physical well-being with the complete absence of any symptoms or signs of ill-health or disease, with strong heart and lungs, perfect functioning of all the organs, nerves, glands, sinuses, and systems of the entire body; firm strong muscles, bones and joints; smooth, healthy, elastic skin, and the absence of any excess fat or flesh; greatly increased resistance to all forms of infection or allergy, and increasing control of both the nervous system and the hormone gland system which, between the two of them, control all the functions and conditions of the body.

Good health not only means physical health but also a healthy attitude of mind in which the nerves are stronger and steadier, the mind calm and clear; more composed; more tranquil; more relaxed; more confident.

It can mean a greater feeling of Self-Esteem; a greater feeling of significance in the eyes of others; a greater feeling of competence in your own eyes; a greater feeling of personal well-being, safety, security and happiness than you have felt for a long time. It can mean complete control of your thoughts and emotions with the ability to concentrate better and utilize all the vast resources of the memory and the intellectual powers of the sub-conscious mind. It can mean the ability to go to sleep quickly and easily at night and to sleep deeply and refreshingly; and to awake in the morning feeling calm, relaxed, confident and cheerful and ready to meet all the challenges of the new day with boundless energy and enthusiasm.

The words "good health" can mean to you any or all of these things and more. These words have tremendous power. I want you to let them sink deeply into your sub-conscious mind, which always does reproduce in you your dominant thoughts.

Now, I would like you to think of the word "assertiveness". It can mean the ability to express *all* your feelings *all* the time; and to do so in a rational, realistic and appropriate Adult manner, without being aggressive or defensive; without triggering anger or retaliation from others; and without allowing yourself to be manipulated or exploited.

In this way, you no longer build up the tight, knotted, tense feelings associated with the repression of your emotions, but instead find it more and more easy to express your feelings spontaneously without fear or hesitation. To speak more and a little louder; to say what you feel; to express your views; to be able to say "No" when you want to; to be able to ask favors or requests; or to be able to start, continue or stop a conversation.

Assertiveness can also mean the ability to show feelings of affection, appreciation and love, as well as those of criticism and disagreement; and to do so, so regularly and consistently that the feelings which you express are always appropriate and reasonable for the circumstances at *that* time and not the result of a build-up of unexpressed feelings over a long period. Repression of feelings causes tension and illness. Expression of those feelings liberates the tension and sets you free to live a healthier and happier life.

Now, I would like you to consider the word "happiness". It can mean first, feeling right with yourself, then feeling right with those around you, and feeling right with your surroundings.

It is not achieved by wealth, power or position, but is found in the process of personal growth and the gradual building of a sense of Self-Esteem, Self-Acceptance, Self-Confidence.

It is found in the process of becoming a fully mature person, capable of dealing with and adapting to his or her surroundings without disharmony of body, mind or emotion. Happiness is love, love of life, love of people, love of challenge. The word happiness is one which has strong emotional significance. It, therefore, has a very powerful effect upon the sub-conscious mind.

Now, I would like you to think of the word "success". It may mean a sense of recognition, satisfaction and achievement in your chosen field in life; a happy, fulfilling sex life; a closely knit, loving family circle; the ability to make firm friends and mix easily in a social setting, or the confidence and skill to speak well in public. It may mean the ability to set and achieve goals in life which are realistic, worthwhile and progressive; and the motivation and determination to achieve those goals. It may mean the confidence to enable you to throw off your inhibitions, to be spontaneous, to express your feelings without fear or hestitation. It could mean the ability to overcome some particular problem; perhaps even some problem about which I do not know. Whatever the word "success" means to you I want you to use this word as an emotional stimulus to produce in you all the feelings which go with success.

Finally, I want you to think of the word "motivation". What can it mean? It can mean the desire, determination and driving force to achieve a certain objective. It can mean a gradual but progressive strengthening of one's desire to be in charge of one's life; to destroy the old recording of habit patterns; to play new music instead of old; to cease being a puppet of one's early conditioning and to become a creator of a new, healthy, happy, successful script in the play of life.

It can mean the gradual but progressive building of a stronger and stronger desire to lose weight, (stop smoking, etc.), until the desire is so great that it is much stronger than the desire to eat (or smoke, etc.), and there is, therefore, no difficulty, hardship or discomfort in losing weight (stopping smoking, etc.).

We have all been conditioned, since birth, to associate words with feelings. Words are, therefore, the tools which we are going to use to produce the feelings and results which we want, and these words are health, assertiveness, happiness, success and motivation."

This approach was first initiated when a patient commented upon the fact that certain words which I had used such as "exactly" or "precisely" had set too high a standard for him. I, therefore, dropped the authoritarian approach and now, almost exclusively, allow the patient to choose, from the material which I present to him, that which he needs. According to the circumstances, I may also soliloquize about such words as "autonomy", "wealth", etc., but I have given in some detail the wording for "health", "assertiveness", "happiness", "motivation" and "success" to illustrate the mode of presentation which I have found most successful.

SOME FURTHER APPLICATIONS OF HYPNOSIS

It is not my intention in this book to produce an exhaustive study of hypnosis as there are many excellent textbooks devoted entirely to this subject. However, there are several other aspects of the application of hypnosis which I would like to include, which may not be found in some of the other texts.

The relief of pain

In such conditions as migraine, tension headaches, dysmennhorea, childbirth, and in the pain associated with terminal cancer, the following simple method may be found to be very effective. After having induced a state of deep relaxation, I will say, "I am now going to pick up your right wrist with my finger and thumb and slowly raise it into the air, and as I do so you will feel it getting lighter and lighter until it feels quite weightless as if it were floating like a feather on the breeze." I then gradually allow my finger and thumb to slip off their wrist as I feel them taking the weight of their own arm. I then continue, "And as you feel your hand floating effortlessly above your head you will feel the blood beginning to drain out of your hand and down your arm and you will feel your fingers and your hand becoming first tingly, and then numb . . . . . more and more tingly and numb . . . . . and when your hand is quite tingly and numb I want you to place it on that part of your head (or any other area in which they have pain) and I want you to feel the numbness flowing from your hand into your head taking away absolutely all sensations of pain, tension and discomfort . . . . . feel the numbness from your hand flowing into your head, taking away all sensations of pain, tension and discomfort. And, when all the pain is gone and you feel beautifully relaxed and comfortable, the sensations in your hand will return to normal and you can just let it drop loosely in your lap."

Ego strengthening for children

"You are now so sleepy and comfortable that you will remember everything that I tell you for a very long time; and these things will have a stronger and stronger effect upon the way you think, upon the way you feel, and upon the way you behave. Every day you will feel healthier and stronger in every way. Your resistance to infection will become stronger and you will no longer catch colds or coughs (where applicable). Your skin will become smooth, soft, healthy and elastic, with no trace of itchiness or soreness (in eczema). The muscles in the walls of your bronchial tubes going down into your lungs will become beautifully relaxed. The tubes will open up very widely so that you can breathe in and out every easily, without any wheezing (in asthma).

"Every day you will feel more safe and secure and happy than you have ever felt before. You will feel more secure in the love of your Mommy and Daddy. You will know that *you* are very important. You are very much loved and needed by your family. You will believe more and more strongly that you have the brains, the ability, the intelligence to be able to do whatever you want to do which is good for you.

"Every day you will find that your school work is becoming easier and more fun, that you understand everything more quickly and more fully, that you remember everything more clearly and easily than you have ever done before.

"Every day you will find that it is becoming easier and easier to express your feelings, to speak up clearly and to stand up for yourself as you have never done before. Every night you will go to sleep quickly and easily and you will sleep very deeply so that you will wake in the morning feeling very healthy and happy."

Bed Wetting

Following the child's ego strengthening I say, "I want you to imagine yourself getting into a nice, warm, dry bed at night; and I want you to feel that while you are lying in bed your bladder is shut very tightly and it is absolutely impossible for you to wet your bed. Your bladder just will not open while you are lying down, but it will open quite easily if you are standing or sitting on the toilet; but it just will not open while you are lying down. Now, I want you to imagine yourself waking in the morning and feeling very pleased with yourself that the bed is still dry and warm and comfortable. I want you to imagine yourself feeling around in the bed and finding it dry and warm all over and knowing that your Mom and Dad will be very pleased with you for having another dry bed."

Each time the child comes back I ask him to bring a large calendar on which every dry night has been circled with red ink or crayon; and I praise him and congratulate him for his steady improvement.

Post-hypnotic suggestions for induction of self-hypnosis

"Every time you practice this relaxation, either here or at home or anywhere else, you will become much more deeply relaxed and the effect will last much longer. Every day you will have a stronger desire to use this form of therapy for your own good. Any time you wish to use this great power, which you already have, all you have to do is make yourself comfortable, close your eyes and take five deep breaths and every time you breathe *out* you will feel yourself becoming more and more relaxed and comfortable and on the fifth breath you will be very, very deeply relaxed indeed . . . . . one, going down slowly . . . . . two, very relaxed and comfortable . . . . . three, deeper and deeper and deeper . . . . . four, nearly there . . . . . five, very, very deeply relaxed indeed. And while you are in this state of complete relaxation, all the suggestions which I have given to you here, together with any other suggestions which you may have given to yourself, for your own good, will begin to show themselves ever more quickly and effectively and lastingly in all your thoughts, feelings, actions and in your state of physical and mental health."

Termination of hypnosis

"Now I am going to count for you slowly from five back through to one, during which I want you to let yourself get lighter and lighter, so that on the count of one you will open your eyes feeling very calm, relaxed, confident, healthy, and happy; feeling very pleased with the progress you have made so far, and very confident that you can continue making progress throughout the coming days, weeks, months and years, until you are in complete and permanent charge of your state of health, and your life in all its aspects. Five (timed with inspiration) . . . . . four, coming up slowly . . . . . three, lighter and lighter and lighter . . . . . two, nearly there . . . . . one, open your eyes feeling absolutely marvellous."

Self-Hypnosis

Even though it is much easier to be taught hypnosis by a therapist and perhaps have it demonstrated by a person skilled in its use, this is not absolutely necessary. Provided a person reads and understands what hypnosis is, and what it is not, as explained in chapter eight, then all he has to do is make himself comfortable, close his eyes and take a few deep breaths, during which he imagines himself becoming more and more relaxed.

While in this relaxed state he should not try to give himself suggestions because this involves using the conscious mind and activating the Critical Faculty. Just relax and let the sub-conscious mind do what it knows needs to be done. Do not force it. Do not try too hard. Just relax for three to four minutes daily. You will be surprised at the results.

The idea is to make up your mind *beforehand* what you want to achieve in the sessions. It also helps if you *write it down* and study it for a few minutes. Then *relax* and think of anything or nothing.

Reaching out for hypnosis is like reaching for a shy horse — it will back away from you. Hold out your hand and let it come to you. If you do not try too hard you will find it will nuzzle you just as the shy horse will, if you have patience with it.

10

How Important are "Hypnotic Techniques in Hypnotherapy"?

When I began to study hypnosis at the first seminar I attended, we received a somewhat perfunctory introductory lecture on the theories of hypnosis, and this was then followed by demonstrations of techniques of induction, techniques of deepening the trance state, techniques for measuring the depth of hypnosis, techniques for age regression, and great emphasis was placed upon these multitudinous techniques.

In my naivety I accepted these pronouncements as dogma, and in my early days of practice I used the LeCron-Bordeaux (15) scale of hypnotic depth or Ideo-Motor responses to determine the depth of the trance state before proceeding to therapy. To oversimplify it, I equated a "failure in induction" with a failure in therapy, a moderate trance state with reasonably good therapeutic results, and a deep trance state as something which gave every chance of excellent results.

It did not take long for these illusions to be shattered, as I found there was no such clear correlation between depth of hypnosis and therapeutic results. It also became apparent that I was using these various techniques and rating scales more to bolster my own confidence than for any practical therapeutic purpose. If a patient failed to satisfy certain criteria as to depth, this gave me an excuse to class the patient as "unhypnotizable", and therefore, exonerate me from any therapeutic ineffectiveness. During a period of about two years I then had three cases which were so unusual and unexpected that I thought I had better record these in detail because the results of therapy seemed to bear no relationship to the depth of hypnosis and I began to wonder if depth, as such, was of any importance.

Cases showing no correlation between "Depth of Trance" and Therapeutic results

The first case was one in which technically (in the sense of hypnotic technique) it was a complete success, but therapeutically it was an abysmal failure. The patient became somnambulistic during the very first session and yet the results of treatment were unsatisfactory.

The second case was one in which all attempts to induce hypnosis, by every means in the book, proved a complete failure during two frustrating hour-long sessions and yet, by the third appointment, the patient had lost her symptoms. In this case, hypnosis had been technically a failure and yet therapeutically a success.

The third case was of a man first seen in 1970 as an acute anxiety neurosis and after several abortive attempts at "induction" was given up as "unhypnotizable". He was subsequently seen again with the same symptoms in 1973. There were no induction techniques used and no testing for depth and yet a sudden and dramatic improvement occurred in his condition.

The first patient was a 29-year-old graduate nurse who came to me with a history of asthma which she was reported to have had since the age of six months. She gave a history of having been in and out of hospital from between the ages of 6 and 18 months with repeated attacks of asthma and of having been plagued with it ever since. Her attacks had varied in intensity and duration during the intervening years, but at the time I saw her she was having an average of about one or two attacks of asthma per week.

After a preliminary explanation of hypnosis and a demonstration, induction was induced by the eye closure technique and the trance state was deepened by arm levitation, arm rigidity, interlocking of fingers of hands, etc. It was immediately apparent that she was an excellent hypnotic subject, and after induction I proceeded to give her suggestions regarding the control by the autonomic nervous system of all the smooth muscles in her bronchial tree.

The following week I saw her again at which time she reported that she had only had two mild attacks of asthma which she had been able to abort spontaneously by self-hypnosis. On the third session she reported still having attacks but of less severity and easier to control.

As she was such a good subject I suggested that it may be a good idea to perform an age regression to determine the cause of her broncho-spasm. To this she readily agreed. During this age regression (which I wish, to this day, I had recorded) she reported graphically as if she were standing and watching herself being weaned from the breast at the age of six months and put onto the bottle. Apparently the bottle feed was too thick and she choked on it and went into spasm. She was taken into hospital and remembered being given water to drink. After this session she admitted that she had not remembered any of this material consciously and was as surprised and delighted as I was.

The following week she reported no asthma at all. I then went on four weeks' holiday and I did not see her again until I had been back about two more weeks. This time she presented with runny nose, eyes, sinuses, and a "cold" which had persisted for six weeks. I explained to her that a cold could not possibly last six weeks and enquired as to what situations this "cold" had allowed her to avoid. It then came out that she was a Catholic and her husband was a Protestant, and he had signed a document promising to bring up any children as Catholics. She was now pregnant and her mother-in-law was apparently "giving her the gears" about these promises. The cold was allowing her to miss the weekly visits to her mother-in-law and was in actual fact a substitute symptom for the asthma which was still not bothering her. At this point I decided that the hypnosis was a therapeutic failure and that I should use some behaviorist approach, in the form of assertiveness, to enable her to overcome her fear of the mother-in-law so that she would no longer need her symptoms. With a little coaching and play acting she soon learned to deal with the situation and her problems were resolved, but not, however, by the application of hypnotic techniques.

The second case was of a lady of 83 who had severe os-teoarthritis of both hips and was almost completely crippled. Her daughter telephoned me and asked me if I would see her for the relief of pain, but I replied that I did not think I could help her, at her age, because hypnosis was a technique which involved new ideas and new attitudes and my results had not, up to that point, been good with elderly patients. However, she kept pestering me to see her mother and eventually I said I would see her. I started to explain hypnosis to her and it was obvious to me that she was not even listening to me. There was no way that I was going to make her understand the finer points of hypnosis and that I was trying to teach her a technique with which she could alleviate her own pain. She was determined that I was going to "hypnotize" her and take away her pain. I realized that she wasn't paying any attention to my explanation, so I decided to treat her as I would a child and try a permissive relaxation type of induction. I told her to close her eyes, make herself comfortable and take some nice deep breaths and every time she breathed out she would feel herself sinking right down through the substance of the chair and floating away. As I was going through the induction routine she kept sitting up and opening her eyes and making such remarks as, "I do hope this is going to work, Doctor", or "I do hope I'm not wasting too much of your time, Doctor".

Each time she did this I would start again and use a slightly different technique, until at the end of the first hour I was nearly pulling my hair out by the roots in frustration! I had tried every technique in the book but to no avail. However, at the end of the first session I said to her, "During this next week you will find that you will still have the pain in your hips but that it is not bothering you quite so much." She left my office and I hoped that I would never see her again. My heart sank when she reappeared a week later and I spent a further frustrating and completely fruitless hour attempting to induce hypnosis, punctuated by irrelevant remarks from the patient. However, I repeated the affirmation about her pain and sent her home. When she arrived the following week, she had an enormous smile on her face and when I asked her how she was she said, "Do you know, it is a very funny thing, Doctor, but this week I have still had my pain but it no longer bothers me and I have been able to visit and read and crochet and do many things which I have been unable to do for more than five years." Here was a patient on whom all the hypnotic inductions had proved a failure and yet the outcome of therapy was a success.

My third case is one of complete failure of hypnotic technique and therapy followed by success of a "non-technique" technique. This man presented himself in 1970 with a severe anxiety state. He was on masses of tranquillizers and anti-depressants. His history was one of constant conflict within his childhood home. He was so anxious and insecure that he could not go into a bank or store or cope with even non-threatening life situations. He was 28 years old, married to a delightful wife, but determined never to bring children into such an unhappy world.

I tried an explanation of hypnosis, followed by every technique I knew but after about five sessions I had apparently failed because I saw him no more. I heard that he spent some time as a voluntary patient in a mental institution and came out on a large dose of tranquillizers. Several months later, I got a phone call from a druggist to confirm that he could have another prescription refilled and I replied that he should only fill it once more but that the man should then come and see me if he wanted more.

When he came to see me I asked him about himself and he said he was O.K. as long as he had large doses of tranquillizers daily, but he still became unbearably anxious in company, so that he never came to town or visited unless he had to. I told him that I had made a great deal of progress in psychotherapy since I had seen him last and I realized that "hypnosis" with all its techniques of eye closure, arm levitation, etc., were clearly not for him, but that if he could only learn to relax and stay relaxed I was sure that his problems would be solved. Therefore, I proposed that we forget all that "B.S" about hypnosis and just close our eyes and loll in our chairs and take some nice breaths and every time we breathed *out* we would feel ourselves sinking right down into the chair and floating away.

I carried on more in this vein for a few minutes with my eyes closed and my head cradled in my arms on the desk. After a few moments I realized by the sound of his breathing and general sense of relaxation that he had achieved a deep state of hypnosis. I then soliloquized in an abstract way about the possible meanings of certain words like health, expression, happiness and success in such a way that he could not criticize what I was saying and then I asked him to open his eyes. He said he felt wonderful, and he has continued from that day to make real progress.

I maintain that the success achieved with this third patient was not due to "hypnotic technique" but to having shown by my attitude and words that the four conditions of Carl Rogers for successful psychotherapy had been achieved, that is,

1. Self-acceptance. "O.K. I made some mistakes before. Let's forget the B.S. about hypnosis and just relax together."

2. Genuineness. By my attitude I had clearly indicated to him that I was not going to try to "pull the wool over his eyes" any more and that I was just going to do my best to help him.

3. Empathy. I tried to show him by the suggestions which I gave him that I could express his problems in my words to his complete satisfaction.

4. Positive unconditional regard. I had failed with him once but I was not going to give up regardless of what he thought of me and my opinions.

So, we can see from these three cases that hypnotic techniques can be as much a snare and delusion as a help, that results are achieved, not by waving a magic hypnotic wand over people but by making them feel significant in our eyes. Let's face it, not many people do feel significant and this is a great step forward. I am not "knocking" hypnotic techniques as such. They have their place but that place is, in my opinion, not of paramount importance. It may also be that these same techniques impart a sense of power and dependence which is the last sort of concept which we should wish to spread.

I feel the results of hypno-therapy depend not so much on the techniques of hypnosis which I used as on two other factors:

First, the "mind set" of the patient; whether he is in a receptive frame of mind; whether or not he is critical of the therapist and his ideas and techniques; and whether or not he has a strong motivation for the treatment to be successful.

The second factor is the character of the inter-personal relationship between the therapist and the patient. Therefore, I feel that all those who use hypnosis in the course of psychotherapy should evaluate themselves very carefully and repeatedly to determine if the techniques which they do use are for the benefit of the patient and to help the patient to learn to take charge of their own lives or whether they are being performed as a form of ritual which enhances the prestige of the therapist and prevents too intimate a contact or involvement with the patient and his problems.

A fourth case which involved a four-year-old child should, I think, also be recorded. This child was brought to me as a behavior disorder. He had been adopted by his aunt and uncle who had a family of older children. His father was still alive and used to visit him periodically but his mother was dead and the father was having great difficulty in looking after him. The child felt very insecure and not only was presenting a problem with regard to behavior but was having recurring attacks of bronchitis. I had seen the child on a number of occasions and it occurred to me that this bronchitis could be the result of emotional stress and I suggested to the aunt that perhaps we ought to try hypnosis on him to make him feel a little better about himself. She brought him to the office and I asked him what his favorite television program was and he replied that he did not have one. I then asked him if he would like to sit down in the chair and close his eyes and he said no he wouldn't. So I said, "Well, that's O.K. I will sit here and I will close my eyes and your aunt will sit there and she will close her eyes and we will both of us think about how you are going to feel more safe and secure and happy than you have felt for a long time. You are going to know that this is your home, that you are loved very much, that the toys you have been given are your toys; you are going to be able to sleep very deeply without any cough; you are going to feel very much better about yourself; you are going to feel that people like you more; and you are going to like other people more."

I carried on in this vein for awhile and while I was talking he was turning the tap on and off in the basin. He was pulling the telephone off the stand; he was pulling my books out of the bookcase, and apparently paying no attention to me whatsoever. His aunt was eyeing me very strangely. After about ten minutes of this I said goodbye to them and that evening his aunt rang me and said, "When we were in the office today I thought you were crazy but when we got into the car to drive home, John asked me if you had meant what you said. When we got home he told his uncle every single thing you had said to him." I saw that boy once a week for four weeks, at the end of which he had lost his bronchitis and he was ceasing to become any sort of problem with regard to behavior. So it seems that it does not matter whether a person is sitting in a chair with their eyes closed and apparently in a deep state of hypnosis or whether they are tearing around the room pulling books off shelves, turning on taps, or playing with telephones. What *does* matter is whether or not the patient *wants* to hear what you have to say. If there is a strong enough motivation for your suggestions to be accepted, then they will be accepted regardless of the "depth" of the "trance".

11

Assertiveness

When I grew up, children should be seen and not heard. The priest, the vicar, the policeman, my parents, my teachers, my boss, the local squire were all authority figures who told me to "shut up", "sit down", "do as you are told", "mind your own business", "don't think, do as I say". I was not a person, but a thing.

At school, they beat discipline into me, they crammed religion down my throat, they filled me full of knowledge instead of teaching me how to learn. As I grew up, the Behaviorists were beginning to tell me that I must counter this by being aggressive, by being rude to people, by taking out my anger by hitting pillows or screaming. The pendulum was swinging the other way. Rebellion invaded every layer of society. The Teddy Boys, the Hippies, the Yippies, the long hair, the outlandish attire took over in an effort to destroy the old order.

Now, recently, a more moderate attitude is taking hold. Not so much emphasis is being placed on Aggression to counter Repression, but a new word is being used which is, to my mind, a much more sane course, which counters repression but is not aggressive; which expresses feelings but without triggering anger and retaliation from others, and the new word is Assertiveness.

Assertiveness is the quiet purposeful expression of your thoughts, feelings and opinions without being aggressive or defensive and done in a manner and tone such as to indicate that you are not about to be manipulated, bullied or cajoled. The assertive person does not label or attack other people or their opinions. He expresses all feelings which need to be expressed in order to avoid the accumulation of inner tensions which could be caused by "bottling them up". This prevents the Monster in the Child from developing the power to destroy you through either rebellious or repressed behavior. Becoming assertive is a learning process and as such, you can learn to become as assertive as you wish, depending upon the time and effort which you are willing to expend in acquiring the necessary skills.

If you go through life being non-assertive, your feelings of personal worth will be low. You will store up irritation, anger, hostility which will show themselves as physical, emotional, thought or behavior disorders. As you become more assertive, you become more able to stand up for yourself, to do things on your own initiative. You reduce the degree of tension in you and your feelings of self-esteem grow.

I have divided training in assertiveness into four different areas: (1) Dealing with critics and manipulators. (2) Starting, continuing or stopping a conversation. (3) Non-verbal alterations in attitude — "The Motto". (4) Dealing with Specific Life Situations — The Assertiveness Scale.

Dealing with Critics and Manipulators

In the book *When I Say "No", I Feel Guilty* by Dr. Manuel J. Smith (25), he describes a number of excellent ways of dealing with manipulators, which I shall mention briefly:

Fogging. Dealing with criticism or manipulation by "taking the wind out of the other's sails" by agreeing with what he says *but not* with what he means. If I return some defective merchandise to a store, and demand a refund and the clerk says, "We don't give refunds", and I repeat, "I want my money back", this will degenerate into a battle which will end with me being thrown out of the store. If, however, the clerk says, "We don't give refunds", and I say, "I fully appreciate your position, but the merchandise is defective", she has to come up with another reason for refusing my request. When I was writing this chapter, I had just plugged in the kettle to make myself some tea, and I was busy writing when my wife came into the kitchen and the following conversation ensued:

Wife: "The kettle is boiling under the cabinets"
Me: "Yes it is, isn't it"
Wife: "It will warp the wood, you know"

Me: "I fully appreciate how you feel"
Wife: "They are expensive cupboards and they will be spoilt"
Me: "Yes, that's true"

At this point, she was about to assault me when she realized what I was doing and started to laugh.

At about this stage in my study of fogging, I made a list of all the fogging-type sentences which I could find. I collected several hundred of them. I was idly looking at this huge list, wondering how one would ever master so many, when I realized that each sentence was divided up into two phrases and that the opening phrases were, in actual fact, very few in number. I selected fourteen commonly occurring opening phrases and decided that all I had to do was to become very proficient in the use of a few of these phrases and add them to an appropriate follow-up phrase in order to form an almost infinite number of fogging sentences:

Opening Phrases

That's true	I fully appreciate
You are right	I quite understand
You could be right	That's a point
You are probably right	That may be true
I agree with you	That is a problem
I'm sure	That's possible
I can certainly see	That's so

You then add to this the criticism or manipulation you are facing such as: it is irritating; it is annoying; it is difficult for you; this is your policy; you must be busy; you have a problem; (and many more, depending on the manner and form of the criticism).

A few examples are:

I quite understand it is difficult for you
I fully appreciate you have a problem
I agree with you, it is irritating
I'm sure, you must be busy

As you can see, with fourteen opening phrases and many more follow-up phrases these can be combined into an enormous number of fogging sentences until your critic gives up in desperation.

Broken Record: Saying what you want over and over again. Be persistent without getting angry or irritated. Stick to your guns.

"I want my money back"

"Please send for the Manager"

"I am not interested in buying your magazine"

An example of the use of a combination of Fogging and Broken Record occurred to me a short while ago. My electric razor broke down. Having an older one which had also broken down, I decided to take them both to be repaired rather than buy a new one. I took them into an electrical repairman and asked him to fix them for me. He agreed and asked if I would like new cutting heads in them. I replied, "Yes, please, but only in the newer one". The following week I went and picked them up and returned home, having paid for three new heads. When I went to shave, I realized that they were not new heads and that I had been ripped-off. "Damn", I thought.

The next week I returned to the store and the dialogue went something like this:

Me: "I had these razors repaired here last week and was charged for three new heads but these heads are blunt".

Repairman: "Well, I repaired them myself, and I know I put new heads in".

Me: "I fully appreciate what you say, but these heads are blunt".

Repairman: "Well, the new heads come in sealed packets and they wouldn't put old heads in new packets would they?"

Me: "I quite understand that, but these heads are blunt".

This dialogue continued for some minutes until the repairman said, in exasperation, "Well, there is nothing I can do about it". I replied, "In that case, the only thing I can do is send the heads to the manufacturer and ask him to examine them under a microscope and send me a report as to whether they are new heads or blunt heads". "Just a minute", he replied, "I will wash them off so that you can see them properly and you can examine them under my microscope". He took the heads into a back room and came out with three obviously new heads, dripping with water, and a microscope. I examined them under the microscope and said, "Well, they look alright, but they are blunt".

At this point, he turned his eyes beseechingly to heaven and said, "O.K. I will open a new head in a sealed packet right in front of you for you to compare it with your heads, but I won't be able to sell this once the packet is opened. I then compared the new head with the others, agreed that they looked the same, thanked him very much and walked out with the three new heads. I now enjoy myself every time I shave whereas I would have hated myself if I had not been sufficiently assertive to get what I had paid for.

Negative Assertion. Coping with criticism which is undoubtedly true by agreeing with what your critic says *and* with what he means, but without allowing your error or defect to make you feel guilty. You accept the fact that you are not perfect (who is?) and agree with what he says without being emotionally upset by the criticism.

"You're right, I wasn't too clever in doing that."

"I've noticed that myself, I am weak in that area."

"That was a stupid thing for me to do."

In this way you rob the other person of the power to hurt you. If a person comes storming into my office and says, "You are a stupid, ignorant, so-and-so", I could reply with my Child and punch him in the nose or I could reply with my Parent and say, "How dare you speak to me in that manner!" In neither case would we have solved anything, and we would both feel bad. On the other hand, I can use negative assertion and say, "Yes, I am aren't I! Take a seat. Now, what is your problem?" He has not hurt me in the least, I have blunted his criticism and we may even resolve our differences.

Negative Inquiry. Active prompting of criticism to either blunt that criticism or obtain useful information on how you are compromising the relationship. For example,

Him: "I am really angry with you."

Me: "What, specifically, has made you angry?"

Him: "Your manner is so superior."

Me: "In what way do I appear superior?"

Him: "You always talk as if you know everything."

Me: "Is it my tone of voice or what I say which upsets you?"

This sort of interchange diffuses potentially harmful situations and may give one or both of you a significant insight into a habit or mannerism which is unnecessary or of which you may be totally unaware.

Workable Compromise: Sometimes a situation arises in which you feel that you are being manipulated by a friend or relative and you don't want to respond with a flat "No". In this case it is reasonable to suggest an alternative solution which will avoid you being "used", but will not cause the other to feel hostile or frustrated. For example, "Will you baby-sit for me this evening?". "No, but I will ask my next-door neighbor if she can."

Starting, continuing or stopping a conversation

Many non-assertive people find that starting and continuing a conversation with strangers can be extremely difficult. To make it easy, it is necessary to be aware of two things:

1. People give away a lot of information about themselves without actually being asked. It may be in their dress (ski jacket, hockey jacket, hiking boots, Masonic badge, blazer badge, Regimental tie, etc.) but is more often in what they say. This is what Dr. M. J. Smith called *Free Information*. If you watch and listen carefully for free information, this gives you many things which you can talk about.

Examples of free information are:
  I do ceramics
  I love scuba diving
  I do surfing with my husband
  I am in the interior decorating business
  I am studying for . . . . .
  I love music

When a person gives you free information, the object is to get to learn more about the person giving the information rather than the subject mentioned. "I love scuba diving" could be answered by "Tell me about scuba diving" or "What makes *you* love scuba diving so much". The latter approach is much more likely to give you a better understanding of the person (which is the aim of communication) rather than details of scuba diving, which may not interest you at all.

2. For each bit of free information, you should try to give some *Self Disclosure* to prevent the conversation turning into an

interrogation. This can be divided into expressions of feeling, thinking, fact, opinion.

"I am studying language and art"

"I love collecting gems, furniture, stamps"

"I am not very good at that"

"I do have lots of faults"

"I have a hang-up about that"

"I am not interested in . . . . ."

"I feel the same as you do"

"I haven't decided yet"

"Frankly, I don't care for . . . . ."

"I feel uncomfortable"

"I feel worried"

"I feel angry"

Stopping a conversation

Sometimes it is necessary to stop a conversation when a person will just not stop talking. To allow yourself to wait, wishing they would stop talking, is not enough, and is apt to make you feel frustrated and, therefore, re-charge your Monster. It is sometimes necessary to interrupt their conversation with such sentences as, "Well it was nice talking to you", "I really have to go now", "Thank you for dropping in", or non-verbally by opening the door for them or getting up out of your seat, or helping them on with their coat.

All the techniques mentioned above are ways of expressing or asserting your feelings so that you do not allow negative charges to build up in your Monster. If your Monster is not charged up it does not have the power to destroy you and you are free to live your life, according to your standards, your beliefs, your moral codes and no one else's.

Non-Verbal Alterations in Attitude — "The Motto"

Under certain circumstances it is both unwise and unnecessary to express angry feelings openly. If you have to deal with or live with people who are totally unreasonable (a boss, a wife, a husband, an in-law) sometimes it is necessary to have a safety valve in being able to express your feelings to yourself.

I remember one instance of a spinster of 58 years of age who had a severe duodenal ulcer. Despite my best efforts with antacids, tranquillizers, anti-spasmodics, bland diets, and bed rest her condition was deteriorating and I thought she may be faced with the possibility of surgery. She was sitting in my office, bolt upright in her chair, knees firmly together, mid-calf skirt (in the era of the mini skirt), hair back in a bun, hands primly clasped in her lap. She began to tell me in a tremulous voice about how she would go to work in the morning and by about 11 a.m., her boss would begin complaining, badgering, criticizing, interrupting work she was already doing to get her to do something else. By noon, her abdominal pain was quite marked. By five p.m. it was severe. She was afraid of speaking up because it is not easy for a 58-year-old spinster to get a new job. By the time she went home and cooked her supper, she could not eat it and she sometimes vomited. She would spend the evening sipping milk and eating "Tums" until she went to bed. Then she would not sleep and she would toss and turn until about 3 a.m., when she would drop into a deep sleep, only to be wakened by the alarm at 7 a.m., to begin yet another day.

I could tell by the way she was sitting and by the way the knuckles were showing white on her clasped hands that she was as tight as a bow string. I adopted a very relaxed attitude in my chair, leaned on my desk and the following exchange occurred:

Me: "You know, my dear, I think everyone should have a motto."

Spinster: "What you you mean?"

Me: "Some sort of jingle or catch phrase which you can say to yourself when people are getting on your back; when things are piling up; when you know you cannot even be assertive without risk and yet you have to let off steam somehow."

Spinster: "What sort of motto do you think I ought to have, Dr. Gorman?"

Me: Looking her straight in the eyes: "Fuck 'em all!"

Her eyes popped out on stalks, her mouth dropped open, and for a moment I thought she was going to walk out on me. Then she started to laugh. First a slow smile, then a giggle and finally a huge belly laugh. Tears streamed down her face and I thought she would never stop. I could just as easily have said to her, "Don't let your boss put you down", but it would not have had nearly the impact of "Fuck 'em all", which acted as a psychotherapeutic shock treatment.

The next week when she came to see me she was much better. She giggled and said that she was using the motto. After about four weeks she came and sat in the chair in a relaxed attitude and told me that she had not had any pain for about two weeks, she was eating better, and sleeping better. She smiled at me impishly and said, "Do you know what cured me? When my boss starts getting on my back, I look him straight in the eye, smile inwardly and say to myself "Fuck you", and I can take whatever he has to dish out without it upsetting me because I know that he is either in his Parent or Child ego state and I have robbed him of the power to make me sick.

Two months later I re-X-rayed her stomach and duodenum and the ulcer had healed. This simple change in attitude, even though accomplished by unorthodox means, which may be considered, by many, to be in bad taste, had resulted in the cure of an ulcer which had defied the best efforts of traditional medicine for nearly two years. Assertiveness, therefore, does not have to be observed to be effective.

Dealing with Specific Life Situations — The Assertiveness Scale

The following list is designed not only to test your degree of assertiveness, but also to give you exercises to practice to become more assertive. If you can answer "yes" to all the questions, then you are already a very assertive person. Any question which you answer with a "no" tells you what area you need to practice.

Are you able to:

1. Change a dollar (five dollars) in a store without buying anything? The non-assertive person buys a packet of gum. If the salesperson gives you change, say "thank-you", and walk out. If he grumbles about "not being a bank", or something like that, say "thank-you very much" and walk out. Do not buy anything to placate him or you are being manipulated.

2. Act "the fool" at a party? The non-assertive person finds it

difficult to put on a paper hat or blow whistles, etc. He simply cannot make an ass of himself in front of others.

3. Dance the modern dances without feeling self-conscious? The best way to deal with this situation is to get someone to show you a number of variations to the common steps so that you do not need to feel more inept or clumsy than anyone else on the floor.

4. Send back a cup of coffee which is too cold, cracked or dirty and ask politely for a replacement? The non-assertive person would leave it and feel bad about paying for a coffee which he could not drink.

5. Tell the hairdresser to change the way in which he or she is doing your hair? Many people will go home fuming and re-do it themselves.

6. Stop people manipulating or exploiting you? Here you would use one or more of the techniques of Fogging, Negative Assertion, Negative Inquiry or Broken Record.

7. Start, continue or stop a conversation. In this situation you would look for opportunities for using those techniques of Free Information and Self Disclosure already mentioned.

8. Tell your parents not to expect you to visit them every weekend? Many people tend to let their parents manipulate them and will go whether they want to or not.

9. Disagree with your boss?

10. Tell an employee or subordinate exactly what you want? Many employers would rather be thought of as "A nice guy" even though it irritates them to be manipulated.

11. Question a grade obtained by your child at school?, for example, "Jane was doing well in grades eight and nine and now she is doing poorly. She is not the only one in her grade who has dropped and I feel the teacher must be at fault."

12. Tell your doctor, mechanic, dentist, etc., you are not satisfied with their services? The non-assertive person pays, grumbles and goes somewhere else.

13. Insist upon your right to judge your own behavior? To the statement: "You should not have done that", you can respond: "I appreciate how you feel, but, in my opinion, that was the correct thing to do."

14. Express your feelings or opinions in the presence of

someone who you think is more intelligent than you are? If you have an opinion, express it regardless of whom you are with. Don't put yourself down.

15. Make a complaint to a government department (or the police) about them?

16. Complain if a stranger (or a friend) gets in front of you in a line-up? The object here is not to precipitate a fight, but to express your feelings, for example, "Excuse me Sir, but there is a line-up here, and I have been waiting some time". If they respond by going to the back of the line, you will feel satisfied. If they refuse to do so, you have at least expressed your feelings and will not be angry with yourself for not having done so.

17. Refuse if an employer expects you to do tasks of a personal nature in your lunch break?

18. Insist upon your right to change your mind? Some people think that to change your mind is a sign of weakness. I feel that it is a sign of intelligence and maturity to recognize when you are wrong and to correct the error.

19. Say "No" or "I disagree" whenever you want and to anyone? It is good practice to say "No" at times just to let people know that they cannot take you for granted. Practice saying "No" to people more often — you can always change your mind and decide to do whatever they have asked if you want to. Practicing emotional exercises is like practicing physical exercises. It is difficult and painful at first, but, with practice, you find that you are getting stronger and the task is getting easier.

20. Cut short the visit of a person who calls on you "for a few minutes", and then looks like staying for hours? People who outstay their welcome are usually thick skinned and insensitive anyway, (or so non-assertive that they do not know how to leave!) Therefore, you can be quite abrupt and suddenly stand up and say "Well, it was nice of you to call" or by helping them into their coat. You will feel much better than if you sat there for several hours wishing they would go.

21. Insist upon your right to be treated with respect? For example, "I feel that you are being disrespectful. Would you please send for the manager?"

22. Ask a friend to lend you money?

23. Ask a friend to do you a favor?

24. Speak loudly enough to be heard easily? Non-assertive people tend to mumble.

25. Ask a friend to stop doing something that bothers you?

26. Ask a stranger to stop doing something that bothers you? Once again, the object is not to cause a fight, but to express feelings so this should be done very politely. If they agree to stop, well and good. If they continue their behavior, you have asserted yourself and need no longer allow their Child response to trigger your Child.

27. Speak up and make a controversial statement at a meeting?

28. Insist upon your right to set your own priorities? For example, "I feel that I should send out the monthly statements before doing the filing."

29. Refuse a friend who asks a favor? Perhaps they may ask you to babysit for them when you have decided to do something else. You agree and feel "used". The deciding factor here is — Do I get a knot in my gut if I agree? If I do, I should have refused.

30. Refuse a friend who asks to borrow money?

31. Use the words "I think" and "I feel" with confidence? Non-assertive people often express their feelings in the form of questions such as "Don't you think we ought to . . . . . ?" In this way, they do not have to take responsibility for their feelings or opinions.

32. Insist upon your right to ask for what you want? You may be having a meal with a large group of strangers when the food is passed around for you to serve yourself. If you didn't get peas or sweet corn and there was a dish on the table six places away, would you ask for it to be passed to you?

33. Be demanding and persistent with all those who are supposed to give a service (salesclerks, taxi-drivers, hotel porters, waiters, etc.)? If given a room in a hotel, over the cocktail lounge or by a noisy elevator, would you ask to be moved?

34. Express love? Some people consider this too "sentimental".

35. Express anger? Many people cover this with a straight face and averted eyes. Anger should be expressed, in an Adult manner,

without allowing your aggressive Child to become abusive.

36. Express frustration? Non-assertive people tend to keep it to themselves and fume inwardly.

37. Express relief? This is often not expressed because we don't want anyone to know how anxious we were.

38. Express appreciation? How much more significant our wives would feel if we thanked them for a beautiful meal once in a while!

39. Express praise? This is an area in which we are often remiss with our children. We complain about their faults, but rarely praise them for their successes.

40. Use facial and hand talk? Non-assertive people tend to keep a "stiff upper lip" at all times.

41. Insist upon your right to get what you pay for? If a tradesman does a poor job installing something in your house, would you insist upon it being corrected before paying? The non-assertive person grumbles to his friends about "shoddy workmanship" and pays anyway.

42. Express agreement and appreciation when being praised? For example,

"You look beautiful in that red dress, Jill".

"Thanks, you have made my day".

Non-assertive people will put themselves down by saying something like, "Oh, I have had this dress for years".

43. Deal comfortably with people who tend to put you down? This can be done either verbally or non-verbally. If the circumstances permit, you can use any of the techniques of Fogging, Negative Assertion or Negative Inquiry. When this is not possible without creating open conflict, you can use "The Motto" (Ch. eleven) to avoid creating conflict within yourself.

44. Insist upon your right to say, "I don't know". It is better to say "I don't know. I will look it up for you", rather than bluster your way through the situation.

45. Return defective merchandise and be persistent about a refund or replacement?

46. Take a front seat at a meeting or church? If there are vacant seats in the front row and people standing at the back you can be sure that, if you stand at the back, you are joining all the other

people with migraine, ulcers and low self-esteem! You can usually judge a person's degree of self-esteem by where he or she sits in a meeting or church. Personally, after a little practice, I have learned to feel better, as well as hear and see better from the front row.

47. Talk to the most important person at a meeting or gathering? They are probably the most interesting people anyway; and, as they usually have plenty to talk about, you will not have to carry much of the conversation.

48. Insist upon your right to say "I don't understand" and to repeat it if you still don't understand? You may feel foolish, but there are probably a number of other people who still don't understand and they will be glad that you were assertive enough to ask for further clarifications, for example, "I'm sorry, I still don't understand. Would you please explain it a different way?"

49. Admit to mistakes and take responsibility for them?

50. Avoid crossing your bridges before you come to them? Many people worry about all the things that *might* happen. Assertive people take things in their stride and deal with situations as they arise.

51. Act according to your standards regardless of what people think of you? Non-assertive people want everybody to like them. Don't forget, you are unlikely to have more than a dozen significant people in the world — so to hell with the rest! Be yourself. Decide upon your own standards of conduct. If they are not destructive to yourself, or anyone else, do what you decide is appropriate.

52. Act immediately in doing things which are distasteful to you — like writing a difficult letter, or, confronting somebody. Non-assertive people put things off or think of the right thing to say about two hours too late. Gain time to think by fogging, negative assertion, or negative inquiry and then say whatever you have to.

53. Take your proper place in a line-up without being too deferential? Some people are always the last into and out of an elevator, or the last in line for food at a buffet dinner.

54. Pass the meal cheque to a friend if it is his turn to pay, or say, "The bill is $20.00, here is my $10.00" and put your share on

the bill? The non-assertive person picks up the bill and pays it, feeling worse about himself every time.

55. Confront situations which frighten you. Many people become terrified when dealing with lawyers in court or policemen at a road block. They are only people doing their job and there is no need to be intimidated.

56. Refuse a substitute article when shopping for anything?

57. Express feelings without giving reasons for what you feel?

58. Do what you want to without making excuses or justifying your behavior?

59. Break into a small group of strangers at a party? This is a common difficulty, but can be overcome by using a small number of opening statements such as "Hi, I am Brian Gorman and I would like to introduce myself." "Hello, I don't seem to know anybody here, may I join you?"

60. Start a conversation with a stranger on a bus, at a meeting or at a party?

61. Ask someone to make less noise at a theatre or a library? This should be done quietly and politely. If they respond you will feel much better than if you said nothing. If they continue to make a noise, you can let them continue their boorish behavior without it upsetting you.

62. Ask the neighbor to turn down his stereo after midnight?

63. Ask for a date?

64. Refuse a date?

65. Speak in public while standing?

66. Stand up for yourself in dealing with authoritative figures?

67. Be pleasantly, but firmly assertive with your Significant people without putting them down? You should not keep your feelings bottled up with your spouse or children. Neither should you be aggressive and give vent to the frustrations which you accumulate during the day. Your feelings should be expressed quietly, firmly, in an Adult Tone, using eyeball contact and prefaced by such phrases as "I think", "I feel", "It is my opinion".

68. Look people in the eyes when you are talking to them?

69. Adopt an assertive bodily posture — stand erect, sit up?

70. Touch another person without feeling embarrassed?

71. Adjust your facial expression and tone of voice to be in

line with what you say? If you smile when you are telling someone off, or look hurt when you are really angry, you are being non-assertive.

72. Count your change in front of the salesperson or bank teller? If you put it in your pocket and count it later "because you don't want to upset them", you are being non-assertive.

73. Express your feelings in terms of what *I* feel instead of what *You* should (or should not) have done. If someone does something which annoys me and I say, "You should not have done it", that is aggressive. If I say, "I feel that you should not have done it, that is assertive. If I say nothing, that is non-assertive.

74. Have a good belly-laugh if you are amused. Non-assertive people tend to snigger.

75. Accept money for services rendered? Many professional people tend to avoid being paid cash by their clients, or patients, as if they were "above" money. They tend to say, "My secretary will bill you". This is non-assertive.

76. Say "I want" or "I don't want" with confidence?

77. Ask for a raise in pay if you think you deserve one?

78. Ask for a promotion?

79. Contend with being watched while you work?

80. Say "I like" or "I don't like" with assurance?

81. Cope with criticism? This is where you can use your techniques of Fogging, Negative Assertion or Negative Inquiry, e.g. "I understand your point of view". "You are right". "In what way, precisely, am I doing it wrong?"

82. Deal with angry people without becoming flustered? Remember, an angry person is either in his Child or Parent ego state. If you remain in your Adult and once again use Fogging, Negative Assertion, or Negative Inquiry, you will find that you will become adept at dealing with angry people.

83. Act as Master of Ceremonies at a wedding or social function? (Such as a Shower for the Bride)?

84. "Chair" a meeting?

85. Go into a restaurant and ask for a drink of water without ordering food or drink?

86. Accept a spontaneous gift without being embarrassed?

87. Quietly, but firmly, stop anyone trying to force their

religious views on you? For example, "I understand your views and agree that you have a right to them, but I do not wish to discuss my beliefs."

88. Deal pleasantly with a dissatisfied customer?

89. Maintain discipline among your staff without being aggressive or destroying their self-esteem?

You may want to say, "This office is in a hell of a mess. Get it cleaned up by five o'clock. This may come out more destructively than if you overplay the situation by such a statement as, "Holy Mackerel! it looks like a cyclone hit this office. I bet you guys can get it cleaned up by five o' clock".

90. Deal quietly, firmly, and politely with door-to-door salesmen? The non-assertive person tends to be overly aggressive in such a situation because they feel they are safe on their "home ground". This leaves them with the residual effects of anger which will trigger the Alarm Reaction.

Some time ago, I had been treating a patient who was painfully non-assertive. We had discussed Carl Rogers' curious paradox of the effect of Self-Acceptance and we had then examined the Assertiveness Scale. Several weeks later, she came back to see me and she was very excited and said, "When I left your office last time, I told myself that I was going to accept myself as a non-assertive person, who lets everyone walk all over her, who hasn't the courage to stand up for herself, who can never speak in public and many more things. Much to my surprise, I found that I was on my feet talking at the next P.T.A. meeting; that I was not allowing people to manipulate me and that I was much more assertive in every way."

Accepting herself as a non-assertive person had initiated a change in her. The Humanistic Psychologists and the Behavioral Psychologists had always seemed to be poles apart, but here we see that the ability to accept herself *as she was* (A Humanistic Philosophy) had enabled her to become more assertive (A Behaviorist Goal).

We have already seen that the theories of Eric Berne in Transactional Analysis do not differ very widely from the concepts of Stanley Coopersmith in his study of Self-Esteem and that these are only expressing in different terms the philosophy of Altruistic

Egotism of Hans Selye. We have seen that Carl Rogers' conditions for successful psychotherapy differ only in the words used to describe them from the healthy Life Position of Tom Harris. Now we see that even the Humanists and Behaviorists can be made to work side by side.

Read this Assertiveness Scale of 90 questions a number of times and make a mental note of those situations with which you have difficulty. Accept those areas and become more aware of them, for in the very awareness of a problem lies the essence of its own solution. You will find that, gradually, your degree of assertiveness will grow and, with it your Self-Esteem.

12
Gestalt Therapy in Transactional Terms

I feel that I must explain how Gestalt theory and therapy can be, and indeed must be, woven into the fabric of a unified concept. It is vital that I be aware of my feelings, that I maintain contact with reality and that I express my feelings so that they do not accumulate and charge the Monster in me to such an extent that it is able to trigger unhealthy reactions. I must not leave "unfinished business" to clutter up my sub-conscious mind to the extent that it interferes with the reality of the now and prevents me from living my life on a day-by-day or hour-by-hour basis.

Fritz Perls, the founder of Gestalt Therapy considered that if you live your life in the past, you are likely to be depressed or guilty. If you live your life in the future, you will be anxious. Only if you live your life in the present can you be truly happy. Therefore, I feel that it is necessary to take Gestalt theory and therapy and transpose it into transactional terms to show that they are really saying the same things but from two different perspectives.

Gestalt Theory

Perls equated the word now with experience, awareness and reality. Restated in Transactional Terms this could be: Now = experience = awareness = reality = the Adult. Gestalt theory is that people's problems arise from their lack of awareness and from the ways in which they block their awareness (being in their Adult ego state). Transactional analysis could be considered the *rational* or thinking-out of intra-personal and inter-personal relationships. Gestalt focuses on the *feeling* aspects of these relationships.

The second basic tenet of Gestalt theory is that the whole of life is a series of drives or needs which arise out of the background of awareness, assume an increasingly important place in the foreground of consciousness until they are satisfied; and then recede into the background again. For example, I may be driving my car along the highway, enjoying the scenery, or perhaps thinking about what I will do when I get to my destination. Suddenly, I realize my gasoline gauge is showing nearly empty. Immediately, the thought of a gas station becomes more and more predominant in my thoughts until I finally see one and refill my tank. Having satisfied the need for gasoline, service stations cease to be important to me and I may drive another 150 miles without even noticing that I have passed half a dozen of them. In other words, gasoline stations were, at first, in the background of my thoughts until the need for gasoline became strong, when they immediately sprang into the foreground. Having been satisfied they receded into the background again. In this case the Gestalt had materialized and remained important until the need was fulfilled and the Gestalt was "closed" and ceased to cause concern. When needs arise which remain unfulfilled or are only partially fulfilled, we are said to be left with "unfinished business" and the more unfinished business we have cluttering up our awareness, the more anxious and unable to concentrate we remain.

Some of the ways in which proper functioning of the Adult is blocked are:
Projection
Retroflexion
Desensitization
Introjection

Projection

This is attributing to someone else those aspects of my own personality which I cannot accept. If I hate everybody, I will project this as, "everybody hates me". If I am dishonest, I will project this as, "You are dishonest". I would then tend to be aggressive and paranoid. If I can learn to imagine myself having the same qualities as I see in others, then I increase my own awareness of myself, I learn to accept myself *as I am* and, thus, tend to change.

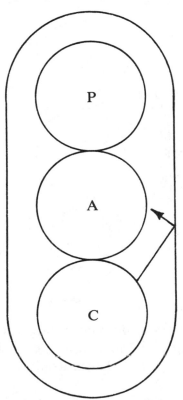

Fig. 12-1 Projections

It is necessary to become aware of what is actually happening around us and to determine if, in fact, our projections are true or whether they are not a reflection of our own feelings about our surroundings.

Retroflexion

This has been described as a conflict between two parts of the personality which involves inhibition or repression of one part but, instead of projecting the resulting resentment, this resentment is turned in upon oneself in order to avoid potentially dangerous conflicts with other people. In transactional terms the Parent is inhibiting the Child through internal dialogue, and the Child, instead of getting rid of the repression, is storing them up and charging the Monster which is bent upon his own destruction.

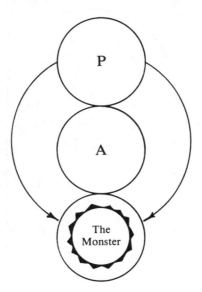

Fig. 12-2 Retroflexion

Without the mass of dogmatic, prejudiced parental material which is continually bombarding the feelings of the Child, retroflexion could not exist. There would be nothing for which to punish oneself.

The most important types of retroflexion are introspection, over-control, and self-destruction.

Introspection. This is the constant examination of one's own feelings and actions in an attempt to avoid arousing conflict with others.

Over-Control. Self-control is necessary to enable us to live in a civilized society. Over-control is the repression of reasonable feelings of anger or resentment.

Self-Destruction. This is constantly seen in the form of excessive humility or "putting oneself down".

Desensitization

Desensitization is a method of blocking awareness, communication, feeling. It is a means of blocking intimacy — for in intimacy one has to risk oneself to allow oneself to be known, to be transparent and genuine, and thus to show one's weak points as well as one's strong. This makes a person vulnerable, a state which most people fear. They, therefore, become desensitized, being polite instead of truthful; and avoid "dangerous" topics of conversation, which might force them to show their true feelings or opinions. In Transactional Terms the desensitized person could be said to be encapsulated.

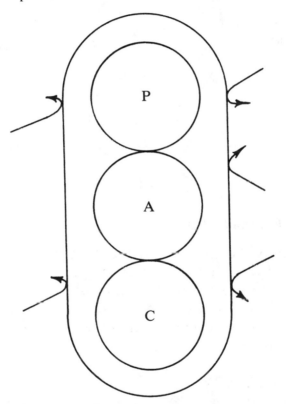

Fig. 12-3 Encapsulated Personality (Desensitization)

Introjection

An introjection is a belief, idea or value system which has been swallowed whole. It has not been digested or absorbed. It is not subject to reason or any form of editing. When changing circumstances cause these value systems to be outmoded, this creates a great deal of conflict within the person. Introjection in Gestalt Terms is very similar to scripting in Transactional Terms.

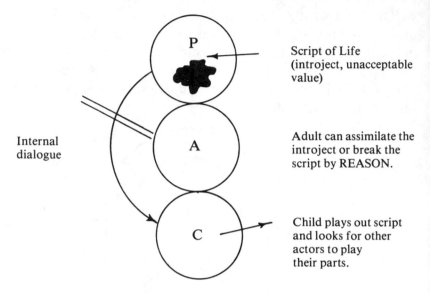

Script of Life
(introject, unacceptable value)

Internal dialogue

Adult can assimilate the introject or break the script by REASON.

Child plays out script and looks for other actors to play their parts.

Fig. 12-4 Introjection

The Aims of Gestalt Therapy

The aim of therapy is to learn to become aware of ourselves and those around us; to feel comfortable with ourselves and our environment, to be aware of the formation of Gestalts and the ability to complete these Gestalts without leaving any unfinished business, the ability to live in the now, which is the only time in which I can be truly happy.

GESTALT THERAPY

Gestalt therapy is divided into a number of specific rules and a very wide range of techniques designed to unblock and allow free expression of feelings. Bringing one's feelings into the open allows them to be examined and expressed in such a way that the destructive forces engendered by them can be eliminated. This allows a person to live an autonomous, script-free, game-free existence. It allows him to be his natural self, to be able to risk intimacy and thus increase his opportunities for self-actualization, for personal growth, increased significance in the eyes of others and increased self-esteem.

Gestalt rules and games were designed primarily for the encounter group setting, but they can be applied on an individual basis as personal exercises.

Rules of Gestalt Therapy

The Principle of the Now.

One of the commonest blocks to awareness is to be constantly harping upon the feelings, thoughts and actions of either the past or the future. What is important is what we are feeling *now*, what is happening *now*, what we are aware of *now*. In applying this rule we have to avoid abstractions and rationalizations. If a person talks about material from last week or last year or early childhood, he must be directed "to be there now and describe how you feel". This can also be done by oneself. If you are troubled by some humiliating experience from the past, go back in your mind and relive the experience, feel as you felt then, try to get the smell, taste and touch of the situation. Bring out your feelings *now*. You may find, quite suddenly, that what seemed terrifying to you in the past may seem quite ordinary and lose its power to frighten you if you can experience *now* feelings you had then.

The I and Thou.

With this we try to drive home that there can be no true communication except between two people. If you talk as if you are speaking to a blank wall or thin air, it, in Transactional Terms, would be an indirect crossed transaction through a third party (in this case thin air or a blank wall). It will inevitably create crosses in the Child ego states of the parties concerned and block intimacy. The "I and Thou" principle is to direct your remarks, through your Adult to their Adult.

You may be surprised and get an Adult-Adult complementary response, such as "I'm sorry, I didn't realize I sounded like that." Whatever response you get, however, you will have expressed your feelings directly. An application of this principle is to practise ad-

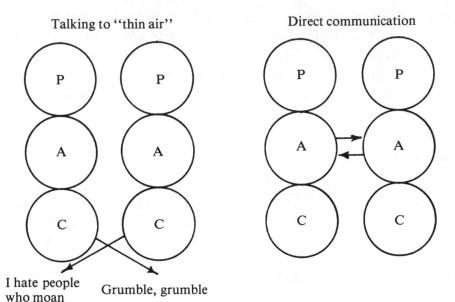

Talking to "thin air"   Direct communication

I hate people
who moan   Grumble, grumble

Fig. 12-5 The "I and Thou" Principle

dressing people by name at the beginning of each sentence to make sure you are making a genuine contact.

"It and I Language".

If I change "it" into "I" whenever possible, I become more aware of my own responsibility for my behavior. If I say "It makes me angry" or "It frightens me" I am implying that "it" has the power to make me angry or frightened. If, however, I say "I am angry" or "I am frightened" then I accept responsibility for my own anger or fear. This is rather similar to when obese people say "I don't have the will power to stop eating" or cigarette smokers say "I don't have the will power to stop smoking". Both of them are refusing to accept responsibility for their actions — implying that some people are lucky to have more will power than they do and it is not their fault that they over-eat or smoke. If they were to say "I don't want to stop eating (or smoking)" this puts the responsibility right where it belongs — on their shoulders.

No gossiping.

This is defined as talking *about* somebody in their presence. This is designed to promote direct transactions between people rather than avoidance of contact, for example, "I don't think John should have done that", should be changed to, "John, I don't think you should have done that".

Changing questions into statements.

Many questions are designed to manipulate others into agreeing with our opinion, but without having to put our own feelings or opinions on the line, for example, "Don't you think we ought to get Jack's crop in while he is in hospital?" should be changed to, "I think we ought to get Jack's crop in while he is in hospital".

Changing "can't" into "won't".

Many people say that they "can't" do something when in actual fact they "won't". I remember once in a group, being told by the leader to "act silly". I replied, "I can't do that". He replied that he could only accept that statement if I replied, "I won't do that". It really brought home to me that I was very unwilling to make a fool of myself in front of the group and I had to take responsibility for my decision not to by saying "I won't " instead of hiding behind "I can't".

Games or Techniques of Gestalt

The Awareness Continuum.

This is a method of helping a person to experience his feelings more completely. He may concentrate on bodily awareness, on what he feels in the way of tension, heat, cold, movement of air on his skin, pressure on his bottom, back or elbows. He can then direct his awareness outside himself to the people and things around him. It is surprising to be in a group doing such an exercise and find that each person reports different experiences and that each person tends to block his awareness of those things with which he is not comfortable. Proceeding further with this exercise, the person should be encouraged to express his thoughts and feelings and to pay particular regard to those areas in which he censors his thoughts. It is not our feelings which cause emotional and physical disorders, but rather the fight to suppress them. If we can allow ourselves to experience our feelings more completely, the repressions (and consequent stress disorders) associated with those feelings become dissipated.

There is another important aspect of awareness training. If I learn to take particular note of my surroundings, then I cannot be worrying about the future or feeling depressed about the past. I should learn to observe people more closely. Are they tall or short, fat or thin, beautiful or ugly, blonde or brunette? What is the color of their eyes, their hair, their skin? Are they well-dressed or slovenly? I should learn to become aware of my surroundings. Are they clean or dirty, plain or artistic, elegant or drab? How do I feel now? Hot or cold? Comfortable or restless? Daily practice in this type of exercise opens up a whole new way of life. Colors become brighter, people more interesting, situations more stimulating. Life is definitely much happier and more fulfilling when lived one moment at a time.

The Empty Chair Technique.

An exercise which I find extremely useful is to place an empty chair in front of the patient and ask him to imagine that his own particular monster is sitting in the chair. I ask him to describe it in detail; I ask him how he feels about it and to express those feelings to the monster.

When he has exhausted his feelings I ask him to change chairs and to become the monster. He is then asked to try to upset himself by being as fearsome as possible. He then returns to his own chair and finds, very often, that this exercise has robbed the monster of its power to upset or frighten him.

I use this extensively in the treatment of phobias, as for example, with elevators and enclosed spaces, with some remarkably speedy and efficient results.

There are many other techniques of Gestalt therapy such as Acting out projections; Exaggeration of gestures, stances, or symptoms, and many more which can be found in any good book on Gestalt therapy and which I will not elaborate here.

I was once attending a Gestalt workshop and one of the group saw someone looking into the window of the room in which we sat. He remarked on it to the group leader who said, "It must be a spy from Transactional Analysis". This remark typifies for me the insular attitude of many people who owe allegiance to a particular "school". I feel that Transactional Analysis and Gestalt Therapy are not contradictory but complementary. Transactional Analysis is the rational approach and Gestalt is the feeling approach and we need both and more.

13
Should
I Join
Group Therapy

The decision whether or not to join a group for psychotherapy is a complex one and depends upon many factors, all of which have to be considered individually before a final decision is made. The following are four of the more important factors.

1. Who is the group leader? Do you know of him or her personally? Is this leader psychotherapeutic or psychotoxic? (Does he establish the conditions necessary for psychological growth; is he ineffectual and does he actually allow destructive games to be played in his group?)

2. Does this particular type of group have some format or structure? Does it have any purpose or sense of direction other than merely to sit in a group of people, all wrestling with their own personal problems and speaking about them when the spirit moves them, as in a Quaker prayer meeting?

3. Is the group one in which *feelings* are the only subject fit for consideration and *rational thought* (or "intellectualization" in group therapy jargon) is considered to be "taboo"? Are there likely to be a lot of pseudo, or false emotions expressed? By this I mean that some group members will often express strong feelings of affection by word, holding hands, embracing, or strong feelings of anger, resentment, or hostility, which are obviously dramatized, excessive, and false. Directed role-playing in which feelings are dramatized or over-emphasized for a specific purpose, is a reasonable therapeutic tool. Structured awareness and sensitivity exercises can be at times extremely helpful. Genuine expressions of

real feelings in a reasonable manner are growth stimulating, but false feelings expressed in an unreasonable manner are destructive.

4. Is there some assurance that if a person allows himself to be completely transparent and expresses his Child feelings and needs, he will be protected by the group leader? If I become completely transparent to the group, I am "leading with my chin" in boxing terms, I am exposing myself in the hope that my needs will be met either by a member of the group or the leader; but I am also making myself vulnerable by such self-disclosure and can have my "Not O.K." feelings intensified by destructive and often vicious crossed transactions by other members' Parent or Child ego states. A group member must have some assurance that any games which he or anyone else starts will be stopped before they become destructive, and the game pointed out to the group for the enlightenment and benefit of all concerned.

My own experience with group therapy has been that if the conditions outlined above can be satisfied, then the group situation can be very therapeutic. However, if they are not satisfied, they can be equally destructive. Those in which there was leadership and some structure shown by the leaders; in which there was genuine expression of real feelings; in which rational thought was not barred but correlated, if possible, with the feelings; in which destructive games were stopped and examined by leader or group; and in which protection was offered to allow a member to disclose himself safely were, in my experience, growth producing. Those groups in which any of these factors were missing I have found to be potentially destructive.

I would like to give as an example a recent therapy workshop which I attended. The leader, whom I shall call Harry, started off by asking each member of the group to introduce himself to the group and to state why he was there and what he hoped to achieve by being there. All well and good so far! However, as the introductions were proceeding I began to notice certain group members who would pounce on anything that was said and make some vicious remark about the person talking. There was no comment from Harry, and each member was allowed to protect himself as well as he could. After the introductions were complete, Harry said that he was going to draw a line on the board which he would like us to think about in relationship to ourselves. Were we on one side of the line or positive about things, or were we on the other side of the line or negative about things, or were we sitting on the line? "Where was our energy?" Although the real meaning of this eluded me and I realized that I had not studied the jargon of therapy enough, I felt that this was probably a reasonable request.

Then began the "revivalist meeting" in which we all sat on the floor in silence, contemplating each other, the ceiling, the floor or a picture on the wall. Then Martin broke the silence with, "I'm all shaky inside." Grace replied, "Why did you take your glasses off when you said that?" Martin: "Because I cannot see you so well and so feel less anxious."

This was followed by a long pause of from fifteen to twenty minutes when the silence was broken again as follows: Ken: "I feel that I am getting a great deal of supportive feelings from the group." Alice: "I resent you assuming that I feel supportive towards you."

I felt that this was a destructive remark directed with calculated accuracy at the "Not O.K." Child of Ken, but it drew no comment from Harry.

After about two hours of silence broken only by sporadic, short and apparently disconnected periods of desultory talk about "where my energy is now", or "I am feeling hostile towards you Carol", Harry suggested that we all take off our glasses and mill around and gaze into each others' eyes. This seemed to be a useful exercise in helping the members to contact each other; and after this the group was a little livelier and there was less of the atmosphere of walking at night in the jungle expecting to be devoured. Then we broke up into small groups without leaders. In my group the following interchange took place:

Carol: "I feel tight in my windpipe."

Brian: "Would you like to try being your windpipe, Carol, and try to express how you feel as the windpipe?"

Carol: "You are being too bloody helpful. I don't want your help. I don't want anybody's help. Besides, you are not my therapist, why should you help me?"

Brian: "That's fine with me."

I realized that I was dealing with a person who was playing

group therapy games. She had deliberately thrown out her "hook" by making the remark about the tightness in her windpipe in the hope that somebody would take it and allow her to satisfy her desire to be destructive. After a few more similar interchanges I realized that this seemed to be the common mode of operation of the group members. Individually, and outside the group environment, I felt that very few, if any of them, would be capable of expressing their feelings adequately. Therefore, in the group, they vented an excessive amount of hostile emotion. They were not taught to express their feelings rationally through their Adult Ego States. In fact, as indicated above, some of them went there with the intention of resisting change, help, or any approach other than of the "where is my energy now" type.

After several more hours of non-productive or even "destructive therapy", Sid, a man with a rather strong, regal face said, "Harry, I am feeling pissed off. I paid fifty bucks to come here and learn something about group therapy from you and all you do is sit there saying nothing. I could just as easily have been sitting at home with some of my friends and it would not have cost me fifty bucks."

Harry: "O.K., Sid, if you feel I am such a bad group leader, you become group leader." He made a motion with his hands and said, "Zap! You are now the group leader. Everybody! Sid is now the group leader." He then carried on with: "Sid, you look sort of regal, I think you should have a court and we should all play parts as members in your court, and as every court must have a jester, I shall be the jester."

It was obvious from this that the group leader was going to make a monkey of Sid for having challenged him, and also that he was giving the other group members permission to destroy Sid. When asked what role I wanted to play I said that I was the ambassador from England and I thought the whole thing was bloody unconstitutional. I said, "Harry, you are not giving Sid the power to become group leader, because everybody knows that you have pocketed the fifty bucks from each of us. You are only putting him in the position in which he can be made fun of and I want no part of it." That ended the charade. I really felt that Harry as group leader was expressing his Child resentment towards Sid, who, in my opinion, had made a valid criticism about the conduct of the session.

After more hours of extreme tedium, a very modified version of Fritz Perls' "Hot seat" was introduced. Several people volunteered themselves for the seat, in which they were the focus of attention of the group and in which they were expected to disclose their feelings. This seemed to be quite harmless until one lady occupied the seat and said, "I feel all shaky inside." Harry then asked her a question regarding these feelings (the precise nature of his question I cannot remember) and she replied with a question. Harry then said rather abruptly, "Don't play games with me", and remained silent. The lady began to weep. Nobody said anything. After a few moments, she said: "I had better crawl back to my corner", and she literally did that amid complete silence. There she remained for the rest of the day. I thought that if she had felt badly about herself when she volunteered herself to be helped, she must feel infinitely worse now.

This kind of thing persisted for nineteen hours in a two and a half day session. I had difficulty in restraining myself from interrupting as I was a group member and observer and it was not my group. However, I felt that for a person to enter that group without a fairly strong Self-Esteem was to put his "O.K. feelings" about himself at risk.

In my opinion, none of the criteria for successful, or even safe, group therapy were satisfied, and this was in a group led by an expert who had been "trained". I shudder to think of all the group psychotherapy sessions which are conducted daily in the mental institutions across the country in which the groups are led by orderlies and almost totally untrained personnel.

Truax and Carkhuff, in evaluating individual psychotherapists, found conclusive evidence to show that if a therapist was not able to establish certain criteria in his relationship with the patient, he not only failed to help the patient but he actually made them worse! Similarly I feel most strongly that if a group therapist does not establish the necessary conditions for successful therapy, then that therapy may well be harmful.

Of all the group therapy sessions which I have attended, usually weekend groups on a Friday, Saturday and Sunday, I have experienced only one which was, for me, a peak experience. This was conducted by Dr. Tom Harris, author of *I'm O.K. — You're O.K.,* in September of 1972.

When I first joined the group, there were 44 other group members and three group leaders, so that the whole could be divided into three smaller groups of 16 members each. The sexes were equally divided but the ages ranged from young nurses of 22 to doctors and probation officers in their mid-fifties. The group was a complete cross section of the "helping professions", plus a sprinkling of interested persons like bored housewives and hippies.

My first reaction was that they looked a crummy bunch, and the prospect of spending fifteen hours with them was not a pleasing one. However, it was an extremely well led group. Part of the time was spent in the smaller groups and the remainder with all members together. We started off by introducing ourselves. Then we had five minutes in which to learn as much as we could about the person next to us and introduce them to the group.

The whole process became so stimulating that after three sessions on the first day from 9 a.m. to noon, from 2 p.m. to 5 p.m., and from 7 p.m. to 10 p.m., nobody wanted to go to bed! We must have stayed in the large hall talking and drinking coffee until about 1 a.m. Nobody wanted to break the spell of the atmosphere which had been established. The next day, we started at 9 a.m. and went until noon, and finished with a session from 2 p.m. to 5 p.m. At this time the course was supposed to end but everybody was still there at 8 p.m.! Nobody wanted to go back into the outside world.

As I drove home, I realized that I could not explain what had happened. I had finished the workshop liking everybody immensely and feeling pretty good about myself, too. I felt that I had achieved a unique experience. I knew that I could not describe this experience to my wife or colleagues — they just would not understand if I went home and said that I had fallen in love with 47 people all at once! It was a growth experience which I shall never forget and is an example of what a well-run group can achieve in the hands of competent and experienced leaders.

Other groups I have attended have varied enormously in their impact upon me. Never again did I experience a really growth producing situation such as I have just described. There were some reasonable groups, but most of them tended to leave me with the feeling that if I had not felt reasonably good about myself at the beginning of the workshop, I would certainly have felt worse about myself at the end. Therefore, if thinking about trying group therapy, pick your group with care!

14
Reality Therapy
in Transactional
Terms

I feel the pioneer work of William Glasser in *Reality Therapy* and other publications, fits into the global picture of a unified concept of psychotherapy, in that the class of individuals which he is treating all come from the reform school setting.

These are the people in whom the repression of the free Child by the external forces of parents, school, church, state, peer group and society have tended to over-adapt the child to such an extent that the Monster in the Child explodes in the form of rebellious behavior. Also, the very circumstances in which they grew up, is such that their chances of feeding the needs of the Child are remote. They suffer psychological deprivation in terms of feelings of significance in the eyes of others and feelings of competence in their own eyes. They never get the chance to feel competent because of the lack of opportunity for worthwhile, growth-orientated activity. They never learn the joy and happiness of true intimacy for who is there that they can trust sufficiently to be completely transparent? Their needs remain unsatisfied and therefore, their feelings about themselves are "Not O.K.".

So, they satisfy their need for stimulation by taking drugs; their need for recognition in the eyes of their peers and of society by acts of violence and destruction; they structure their time with rituals and symbols (leather jackets, motorcycles, tattooing) and by playing destructive games which give them negative strokes at the expense of others. In Reality Therapy, the aim is to make the patient feel significant in the eyes of others. He needs to love and to be loved, he needs to feel competent in his own eyes, and for this he must have reasonable goals and a responsible attitude towards achieving those goals. There are five basic principles of Reality Therapy.

1. **Involvement**

Glasser considers this the foundation of Reality Therapy. The patient must see that another person cares for him. Nothing in life can replace the love of another person. He must feel significant in the eyes of at least one other person in order to be able to let go of his irresponsible, aggressive, destructive behavior. If you can establish the four conditions of Carl Rogers for successful psychotherapy — Acceptance, Congruence, Empathy, and Positive Unconditional Regard, then you *are* involved sufficiently to initiate change.

2. **Current Behavior**

The second necessary condition for establishing self-esteem is a feeling of competence. I must feel worth something in my own eyes. Therefore, the patient has to be taught to examine his current behavior to see if it is making him feel better or worse. He has to realize that he has a choice as to whether to continue with his present behavior or to establish new goals which would make him feel better about himself. The therapist does not judge the patient's behavior but encourages him to compare it with other types of behavior which could be more fruitful. The emphasis should not be on the errors in behavior but on the alternatives which are likely to produce growth.

3. **Planning Responsible Behavior**

In order to do this, the patient must be encouraged to set realistic goals. A person, who has previously failed, needs a series of small, progressive successes in order to build his feelings of competence.

4. **Commitment**

After the goals have been set, these goals must be carried out. If possible it is more effective if an actual contract can be made with the patient, in writing, and signed and dated. No excuses should be accepted for failure to keep the commitment. Accepting an excuse condones the failure and is not likely to lead to success. The therapist should tell the patient that making excuses to the therapist is not going to help him — that only one thing *is* going to help him — the successful attainment of his goals.

5. No Punishment

Punishment reinforces failure. Privileges reinforce success. The earning of privileges for successful behavior is more easily applied in an institutional setting than in private therapy, but the rebellious person does not normally come voluntarily for therapy anyway, so this situation rarely arises.

In studying the foregoing principles of Reality Therapy, it is clearly evident the approach differs very little from that employed in treating the repressed patient. Both need Self-Acceptance, Other Acceptance, Genuineness, Empathy and Positive Unconditional Regard. The only difference is that the repressed person needs to substitute assertiveness for non-assertiveness whereas the rebellious person needs to have his aggressions toned down to a comfortable level of assertiveness, by examining current behavior, comparing it with more productive behavior, setting realistic goals and rewarding success.

15
The
Unified Method
in Action

In order to demonstrate how the principles outlined in this book may be applied to the treatment of psychosomatic and emotional disorders, I am going to present a hypothetical case which I shall work through in the same manner as I do with real patients. The material is drawn from a number of cases and represents quite a large clinical experience in this type of approach. I am including this history in order to allow the reader to follow it through and to be able to refer back to the appropriate sections of the book so that he can do very much what the patient does in therapy. For those who are interested in using therapy of this nature I hope that this case history will be of some use in enabling you to see the manner in which I have been approaching this type of patient.

This was a 34-year-old lady who presented with a history of migraine headaches for twelve years, persistent eczema of arms and legs and recurrent episodes of depression with no apparent cause. She would have two or three severe headaches a week. They were one-sided and accompanied by nausea, vomiting, abdominal pain, and photophobia. She admitted to being a perfectionist in her hobbies but not in housework. Her husband was a self-employed businessman and they worked together in the business. This was something of a strain in that her husband was quite demanding of her as an employee and yet expected her to have their home spotless whenever he brought guests home, which was frequently. She found her husband a difficult man to argue with and therefore,

tended to keep her feelings to herself. Her family history was of being raised by a very narrow-minded, bigoted father and as a child
she had never expressed her feelings adequately. She reported having been thoroughly investigated neurologically to make sure that
there was no organic cause for her headaches. She had tried
numerous creams for her skin and several different anti-
depressants for her depressions — but to no avail. I spent the rest
of this first session explaining the mechanisms of stress and disease
to her (see chapter one) and explaining how I proposed that we attack the alarm phase of the General Adaptation Syndrome with a
combination of relaxation techniques and examination and
modification of attitudes and behavior.

Session 2. This was devoted to an explanation of hypnosis
(chapter eight). I then sent her away with instructions to think
about it and to ring through to the office when she had decided she
wanted to try hypnosis, so that I would be sure that I had not put
any pressure on her.

Session 3. When she returned for this session, my secretary
then demonstrated hypnosis for her and this was done for two
reasons: the first to remove any last vestiges of fear of the unknown
which may remain in the patient's mind, and the second that, if
acting or role playing does play some part in the induction of the
state of hypnosis, then this would give her a role to follow. I then
asked her to take the recliner chair and started with a permissive
relaxation of hypnosis (chapter eight). After she had become very
relaxed, I used the arm levitation technique for the relief of pain
(chapter eight). When her hand felt numb and tingling I told her to
place it on that part of her head where she had her heachaches.
Within a minute she placed her hand on one side of her head and I
told her that she could feel the numbness and tingling flowing from
her hand into her head taking away absolutely all sensations of
pain, tension and discomfort. I told her that when all the pain and
tension were gone the sensations in that hand would return to normal and she could just let her hand drop loosely in her lap again.
Within a minute or so she dropped her hand into her lap and I gave
her direct suggestions for the strengthening of her self-esteem
(chapter nine), and then I gave her the suggestions for producing
self-hypnosis and deepening the trance herself. I brought her out by

counting slowly backwards from five through one. When she opened her eyes she had the most beautiful smile on her face.

Therapist: "How are you, Ann?"

Ann: "I feel absolutely super."

Therapist: "Do you feel nice and relaxed?"

Ann: "Yes, more completely relaxed than I have ever been before. I felt as if I were deeply asleep and wide awake at the same time."

Therapist: "How did your arm feel?"

Ann: "Very light indeed. I was amazed. I didn't think it would stay up there like that but it did, and it did become tingly and numb."

Therapist: "Did the numbness and tingling transfer to your head when you placed it on your head?"

Ann: "Yes, but my head did not become quite as numb as my hand."

Therapist: "That's perfectly all right. This is a learned skill and it improves with practice."

Ann: "By the way, I am a keen scuba diver and I would prefer to imagine pulling myself down the anchor chain instead of going down the escalator."

Therapist: "O.K. We can use that next time."

I then proceeded to describe for her the principles of structural analysis (chapter two), dealing with the Parent, the Adult and the Child ego states and the effect upon the Child of the environment. This took up the balance of the session.

Session 4. Ann came into the room with a very cheerful expression on her face and said, "I had my period last week and it was not accompanied by a migraine for the first time in over four years."

Therapist: "I'm delighted. Take a seat."

Ann: "I have been trying hypnosis at home and I do not feel that I am getting as deeply relaxed as I did in the office here last week but nevertheless, I feel much more relaxed than I was previously."

Therapist: "Well, don't try too hard. This is a learned skill and it comes with practice but you must not try too hard."

Ann: "I forgot to tell you last time that I'm very nervous about flying in airplanes. Perhaps you could give me some suggestions about that this time."

Therapist: "Certainly."

Then we sat and discussed the concepts of transactional analysis (chapter three) with particular emphasis upon the characteristics of the Parent, Adult and Child ego states, so that Ann could learn to spot these states in other people and in herself, and thus learn to stop people having the power to produce a migraine in her. The last ten minutes of the session were spent in giving her direct suggestions in the relaxed state with special emphasis on her skin, the absence of depression and her ability to fly without discomfort.

Session 5.

Ann: "I missed at least three dandy headaches during the last couple of weeks."

Therapist: "Beautiful. Keep up the good work."

Ann: "I flew with my husband to Vancouver last weekened and I didn't have any nervousness in the airplane."

Therapist: "I'm very pleased. You really are making progress."

We spent most of this session discussing the life positions and the five conditions necessary for the establishment of good self-esteem (chapter seven) — significance in the eyes of others; competence in her own eyes; the adherence to reasonable standards of integrity; methods of increasing her assertiveness and her ability to cope with guilt. For this third session of hypnosis I changed the manner of delivering suggestions to the abstract approach (chapter nine), so that I could bring in some of the material which we had discussed in therapy.

Session 6.

Therapist: "Good morning, Ann. How are you?"

Ann: "Absolutely marvellous. I'm much more relaxed now than I have ever been. I haven't had a headache since last week and I seem to be coping much better with life. I have not been nearly so depressed and my eczema seems much better."

Therapist: "Did you find that you were able to sit down and make a list of your significant people?"

Ann: "Yes indeed, and I was very surprised at how small it was."

Therapist: "What conclusions did you come to with regard to your feelings of competence about yourself?"

Ann: "I did realize that I was setting goals which are too high and that really nothing matters enough for me to allow it to produce a headache."

Therapist: "That's the girl. How were you with regard to dealing with guilts? Do you have any guilts of a serious nature?"

Ann: "No, really nothing about which I feel terribly guilty."

Therapist: "How about assertiveness? Were you able to express your feelings somewhat more adequately this week than you previously have?"

Ann: "I may not have expressed myself more assertively but at least I was aware of those situations where I should be expressing my feelings, and this, I feel, is a good start."

Therapist: "I agree with you. Now today we are going to discuss the theories of Carl Rogers and his four conditions which are necessary for the establishment of good inter-personal relationships." (chapter seven).

I went into the explanation of self-acceptance and other acceptance. How we must learn to accept ourselves as we are before we can begin to change. That she must learn to accept herself as a perfectionist but not allow it to bother her any more, not allow it to dominate her life. She has got to learn to accept her husband as he is. At this point she interjected with, "By the way, I think my husband should come and see you too, because I feel that I am leaving him behind in certain respects and I would like him to know more about what we are discussing too. He also has an ulcer and I think this would benefit him greatly. He works extremely hard and is under considerable pressure and I would like him to join in the sessions."

Therapist: "I would be delighted if he would come with you, as I agree that the more we all know of these things the better it is for us."

Then we discussed congruence — being genuine, sincere and transparent. How it does not pay in the long run to put up a false front with other people. That if a person could not accept us as we are it really didn't matter too much, there are always some who could and these are the ones whom we could turn into significant people. Then we discussed empathy or understanding and I suggested that it would be a good idea if she and her husband were to have an empathy session once in awhile. By this I mean that they would sit down in the kitchen and set the timer on the oven for five minutes, and during that five minutes she would try to express in her words how her husband felt and he was just to tell her if she was right or wrong and put her right if she was misinterpreting his feelings about her. (The important point in this empathy session is that during this five minutes any expression of my interpretation of the other person's feelings about me must not be construed as an attack, but only as a searching to reach understanding.) At the end of the five minute session the timer would be reset for another five minutes, during which the process would be reversed and her husband would try and express in his words how she felt about him. This, I feel, is a very valuable exercise for husbands and wives. Sometimes I may feel that my wife is angry with me. When we have an empathy session I may find that, in actual fact, she was worried about something which was not related to me.

This helps to clear the air of many misunderstandings. Ann thought that this was a very good idea and said that she would practise it.

When we discussed the fourth condition of positive unconditional regard, we agreed that if there was self-acceptance, other-acceptance, sincerity and genuine understanding, then it would be difficult not to have positive unconditional regard.

For the last ten minutes of the hour I gave her a further session of relaxation in which I used the abstract approach, and brought into the suggestions more of the material which we had discussed.

Session 7.

Therapist: "Good morning, Ann. How are you?"

Ann: "Just great. It is now the longest period in twelve years during which I have been free from migraine. My skin is now clear, as you can see, and I have not felt depressed for weeks."

Therapist: "Excellent. Keep up the good work. Now today I want to talk about assertiveness". (chapter eleven).

For the next half hour or so we went over the assertiveness scale of 90 questions and rated her on these questions, and found that she was fairly assertive but there were areas in which she was not expressing her feelings adequately. At this point I introduced her to The Motto (chapter eleven) and this produced a delighted laugh from Ann. Once again we had another session of hypnosis, during which we stressed the suggestions with regard to assertiveness.

Session 8. For this session Ann came in accompanied by her husband. She brought with her the diagrams which I had drawn for her during the previous sessions and we spent most of the time going over and reviewing the various items with her husband John, and giving him an explanation of hypnosis.

Session 9. Ann returned again with John and this time we induced hypnosis in John and he seemed extremely pleased with the result. We discussed the part of the chapter concerned with means of dealing with manipulators (chapter eleven). Ann reported that she had had one slight migraine during the preceding week but had been able to abort it by herself by relaxing in the chair.

I then had two more sessions with John by himself and he seemed delighted, not only with the way in which his abdominal discomfort had lessened and the way he was altering his attitude towards his work, but also with the way in which he and Ann were becoming much closer. I did not see them then for a year at which time they reported that they were both in excellent health. She had not had more than three mild headaches during the course of the year and his ulcer had not bothered him in the least. When they came back to see me a year after the end of treatment, it was really to tell me how they had apparently continued to grow in their ability to deal with their life situations and felt that their relationship between themselves had strengthened considerably, and that this was a bonus, as it were, on top of the loss of their symptoms.

John was also pleased to be able to relate a situation to me in which he had expressed his feelings assertively in such a way that he had not been manipulated or bullied. It had occurred when he was having a quick lunch in a cafe. He ordered a hamburger, and having eaten it, he realized that he had time for a cigarette with his cup of coffee. He lit a cigarette. Suddenly the man at the next table half turned towards him and in a loud voice and somewhat aggressive tone said, "I don't think you should be allowed to smoke those in here." John turned and said directly to him, "I fully appreciate how you feel, sir", and carried on smoking. The man said nothing in return, and John had felt very good. He felt that if he had stubbed his cigarette out following that aggressive remark he would have been bullied. If he had carried on smoking without having said anything, he would have been angry and this anger would have persisted long after the episode occurred. John had thus expressed his feelings by using a fogging sentence and had got rid of any repressed feelings without being either aggressive or defensive.

I feel that this case illustrates quite clearly that if I had sat and listened to Ann for this number of sessions without contributing very much in the way of discussions of attitude and behavior, we would not have achieved as much as we had in such a short period of time. If I had just limited myself to paraphrasing her to help her understand that she was being understood, little would have been accomplished. I feel this active, directive approach in which we examined her attitudes and behavior is much more conducive to achieving rapid results than other forms of psychotherapy. In seven sessions with Ann, two joint sessions and two sessions with John, we had been able to treat her previously intractable migraine and eczema, she had ceased to be depressed, she had lost her fear of flying, John had lost his abdominal pains, their marriage was on firmer ground and they both reported that they felt they were continuing to grow and mature long after the end of therapy.

16
Results
of Therapy

A short while ago it began to be apparent that my rather unorthodox method of therapy was producing some surprising and unexpected results. The combination of Relaxation Techniques, accompanied by Ego-Strengthening, plus the examination, discussion and modification of the attitudes and behavior of the patient, all within a therapeutic relationship which had certain clearly defined characteristics, was producing more than just the relief of symptoms.

I began to think that there was perhaps more to the method than I had realized, so I sent out a questionnaire (Appendix C) to a number of patients whom I had treated in this manner to try to find out more definitively what was happening.

The results of therapy were evaluated by sending out the questionnaire to 283 patients who had been treated by the methods outlined in this book, and each of these must have had five or more sessions. 47 failed to reply and 236 replied (84.4%).

Each patient was assigned a number, to maintain anonymity. The purely emotional disorders (anxiety, depression, low self-confidence, etc.) were classed together, and of these there were 93. The psychosomatic disorders were treated separately to give a more accurate picture of those conditions seen most commonly and those which responded best.

Combined Results

Number of patients seen: — 236

Presenting symptoms: — Emotional and psychosomatic symptoms

Average time since end of therapy: — 14.3 months

Average number of sessions per patient: — 7.7

Percentage taking regular medication before therapy: — 45%

Percentage taking regular medication 14.3 months after therapy: — 14%

Of those taking medication after therapy 11 patients reported taking smaller amounts and less frequently.

Question (1) How were you are the end of treatment?

Complete loss of symptoms 12%

Very improved 66%

Slightly improved 20%

No change 2%

Worse .... Nil

Question (2) Had your attitude towards yourself changed during treatment?

Very improved 66%

Slightly improved 30%

No change 4%

Worse .... Nil

Question (3) Had your attitude to coping with life situations changed?

Now able to cope with anything 12%

Very improved 61%

Slightly improved 25%

No change 2%

Worse .... Nil

Question (4) How are you now?
 Continuing to improve in your ability to cope 56%
 Maintaining the improvement 39%
 No change 3%
 Worse 2%

Question (5) What, in your opinion, were the factors most important in therapy?
List 1-4 in order of importance. 11 patients failed to comment. 5 rated them of equal value. 220 made a definite choice.

	1st Choice	2nd Choice	3rd Choice	4th Choice	
Attitude Modification	80	69	52	19 =	220
Behavior Modification	32	48	58	82 =	220
Hypnosis	59	55	46	60 =	220
Character of the relationship	49	48	64	59 =	220
	220	220	220	220	

Emotional Disorders

Number of patients seen: — 93

Presenting symptoms: — Anxiety, depression, phobias, lack of confidence, post-partum depression and panic attacks.

Average time since end of therapy: — 12.6 months

Average number of sessions per patient: — 7.8

Percentage taking regular medication before treatment: — 36%

Percentage taking regular medication 12.6 months after end of treatment: — 11%

Of those taking medications after therapy six patients reported taking smaller amounts and less frequently

Question (1) How were you at end of treatment?

Complete loss of symptoms	3%
Very improved	70%
Slightly improved	24%
No change	3%
Worse	Nil

Question (2) Had your attitude towards yourself changed during treatment?

Very improved	68%
Slightly improved	29%
No change	3%
Worse	Nil

Question (3) Had your attitude to coping with life situations changed?

Now able to cope with anything	11%
Very improved	61%
Slightly improved	28%
No change	Nil
Worse	Nil

Question (4) How are you now?

Continuing to improve in your ability to cope 58%

Maintaining the improvement 37%

No change 3%

Worse 2%

Question (5) What, in your opinion, were the factors most important in therapy? List 1-4 in order of importance. 2 Patients failed to comment on this question. 4 patients rated these factors of equal importance. The remaining 87 patients made choices as indicated.

	1st Choice	2nd Choice	3rd Choice	4th Choice	
Attitude Modification	32	22	22	11 =	87
Behavior Modification	13	18	20	36 =	87
Hypnosis	21	24	17	25 =	87
The Character of the Relationship	21	23	28	15 =	87
	87	87	87	87	

Psychosomatic Disorders
Migraine and Tension Headaches
Number of patients seen: 69
Average time since end of treatment: 12.8 months
Average number of sessions per patient: 7.5
Percentage of patients taking regular medication before therapy: 46%
Percentage of patients taking regular medication 12.8 months after therapy: 16%
Of these, two reported taking smaller amounts less frequently.

Question (1) How were you at end of treatment?

Complete loss of headaches 14%
Very improved 61%
Slightly improved 23%
No change 2%
Worse .... Nil

Question (2) Had your attitude towards yourself changed during treatment?

Very improved 62%
Slightly improved 32%
No change 6%
Worse .... Nil

Question (3) Had your attitude to coping with life situations changed?

Now able to cope with anything 9%
Very improved 62%
Slightly improved 26%
No change 3%
Worse .... Nil

Question (4) How are you now?

Continuing to improve in your ability to cope 53%
Maintaining the improvement 41%
No change 3%
Worse 3%

Question (5) What, in your opinion, were the factors most important in therapy? List 1-4 in order of importance. 4 patients made no comment on this question. The remaining 65 patients made choices as indicated.

	1st Choice	2nd Choice	3rd Choice	4th Choice	
Attitude Modification	23	23	16	3 =	65
Behavior Modification	7	15	19	24 =	65
Hypnosis	21	16	12	16 =	65
The Character of the Relationship	14	11	18	22 =	65
	65	65	65	65	

Psychosomatic Disorders

Asthma

Number of patients seen: 12

Average time since end of treatment: 25 months

Average number of sessions per patient: 9.5

Percentage of patients taking regular medication before therapy: 75%

Percentage of patients taking regular medication 25 months after therapy: 17%

Of these, two patients reported taking smaller amounts and less frequently.

Question (1) How were you at end of treatment?

Complete loss of symptoms 17%

Very improved 75%

Slightly improved 8%

No change .... Nil

Worse .... Nil

Question (2) Had your attitude towards yourself changed during treatment?

Very improved 50%

Slightly improved 42%

No change 8%

Worse .... Nil

Question (3) Had your attitude to coping with life situations changed?

Now able to cope with anything 8%

Very improved 67%

Slightly improved 17%

No change 8%

Worse .... Nil

Question (4) How are you now?

Continuing to improve in your ability to cope 58%

Maintaining the improvement 42%

No change .... Nil

Worse .... Nil

Question (5) What, in your opinion, were the factors most important in therapy? List 1-4 in order of importance.

2 patients made no comment on this question. The remaining 10 patients made choices as indicated.

	1st Choice	2nd Choice	3rd Choice	4th Choice	
Attitude Modification	2	4	3	1 =	10
Behavior Modification	3	2	2	3 =	10
Hypnosis	2	3	3	2 =	10
The Character of the Relationship	3	1	2	4 =	10
	10	10	10	10	

Psychosomatic Disorders

Eczema and Allergy

Number of patients seen: 11
Average time since end of treatment: 22.9 months
Average number of sessions per patient: 6.6
Percentage of patients taking regular medication before therapy: 54%
Percentage of patients taking regular medication 22.9 months after therapy: 9%

Question (1) How were you at end of treatment?
    Complete loss of symptoms 27%
    Very improved 55%
    Slightly improved 18%
    No change .... Nil
    Worse .... Nil

Question (2) Had your attitude towards yourself changed during treatment?
    Very improved 91%
    Slightly improved .... Nil
    No change 9%
    Worse .... Nil

Question (3) Had your attitude to coping with life situations changed?
    Now able to cope with anything 27%
    Very improved 55%
    Slightly improved .... Nil
    No change 18%
    Worse .... Nil

Question (4) How are you now?

Continuing to improve in your ability to cope 54%

Maintaining the improvement 46%

No change .... Nil

Worse .... Nil

Question (5) What, in your opinion, were the factors most important in therapy? List 1-4 in order of importance. All 11 patients answered this question.

	1st Choice	2nd Choice	3rd Choice	4th Choice	
Attitude Modification	4	5	2	0 =	11
Behavior Modification	2	2	3	4 =	11
Hypnosis	4	2	2	3 =	11
The Character of the Relationship	1	2	4	4 =	11
	11	11	11	11	

Psychosomatic Disorders

Peptic Ulcers

Number of patients seen: 11

Average time since end of treatment: 10.5 months

Average number of sessions per patient: 7.5

Percentage of patients taking regular medication before therapy: 63%

Percentage of patients taking regular medication 10.5 months after therapy: 18%

Of these, one patient reported taking less medication than before.

Question (1) How were you at end of treatment?

Complete loss of symptoms	18%
Very improved	64%
Slightly improved	18%
No change	Nil
Worse	Nil

Question (2) Had your attitude towards yourself changed during treatment?

Very improved	64%
Slightly improved	36%
No change	Nil
Worse	Nil

Question (3) Had your attitude to coping with life situations changed?

Now able to cope with anything	27%
Very improved	46%
Slightly improved	27%
No change	Nil
Worse	Nil

Question (4) How are you now?
Continuing to improve in your ability to cope 64%
Maintaining the improvement 27%
No change 9%
Worse .... Nil

Question (5) What, in your opinion, were the factors most important in therapy? List 1-4 in order of importance. All 11 patients answered this question.

	1st Choice	2nd Choice	3rd Choice	4th Choice	
Attitude Modification	7	2	2	0 =	11
Behavior Modification	2	4	1	4 =	11
Hypnosis	0	3	4	4 =	11
The Character of the Relationship	2	2	4	3 =	11
	11	11	11	11	

Assorted Psychosomatic Disorders

Menstrual pains (4), Crohn's disease* (3), Hair pulling (2), Difficulty in swallowing (4), Unstable diabetes (2), Addiction to Heroin (1), Claustrophobia (1), Alcoholism (2), Travel sickness (2), School drop-out (1), Numbness (1), Impotence (2), Bedwetting (1), Chest pains (3), Trigeminal Neuralgia (1), Nervous Colitis (4), Muliple symptoms (6).

Number of patients seen: 40
Average time since end of therapy: 15.8 months
Average number of sessions per patient: 7.9
Percentage of patients taking regular medication before therapy: 47%
Percentage of patients taking regular medication 15.8 months after therapy: 17%

Question (1) How were you at the end of treatment?

Complete loss of symptoms	20%
Very improved	65%
Slightly improved	12%
No change	3%
Worse	Nil

Question (2) Had your attitude towards yourself changed during treatment?

Very improved	67%
Slightly improved	30%
No change	3%
Worse	Nil

Question (3) Had your attitude to coping with life situations changed?

Now able to cope with anything	12%
Very improved	63%
Slightly improved	22%
No change	3%
Worse	Nil

Question (4) How are you now?

Continuing to improve in your ability to cope 55%
Maintaining the improvement 42%
No change 3%
Worse .... Nil

Question (5) What, in your opinion, were the factors most important in therapy? List 1-4 in order of importance. 3 patients failed to comment, one rated these factors of equal importance. 36 made a definite choice.

	1st Choice	2nd Choice	3rd Choice	4th Choice	
Attitude Modification	12	13	7	4 =	36
Behavior Modification	5	7	13	11 =	36
Hypnosis	11	7	8	10 =	36
Character of the Relationship	8	9	8	11 =	36
	36	36	36	36	

*Crohn's disease is an inflamation with ulceration of the terminal ileum. Three cases were treated by psychotherapy. Two have remained clear for 3 years and 18 months respectively, the third remained unchanged. Whether or not they were cases of spontaneous remission (which may occur) is a matter of conjecture.

Question (4) The answers to the questions: "How are you now?" are indeed illuminating. If each of the answers to this question are totalled, it shows that, 14.3 months after the end of therapy:

133 are continuing to improve in their ability to cope .. 56.4%
91 are maintaining the improvement 38.6%
7 are unchanged 3.0%
5 are worse 2.0%

This seems to indicate that improvement does not cease with the termination of therapy but, in the overall majority (56.4%), it initiates a self-perpetuating movement in the direction of growth and maturation. In other words, the results showed that this method of therapy was not like a pill or a shot in the arm, but was the start of an on-going process which would, hopefully, continue throughout life. This was a totally unexpected and exciting finding.

Question (5) "Which, in your opinion, were the factors most important in therapy? List 1-4 in order of importance".
These results were listed in columns with each factor in one column. These were then totalled so that the lowest total would indicate the most important factor, the highest total the least important. Eleven patients failed to comment on this question, five gave equal value to each factor and I have scored them at 2.5 each.

	Ranking Method			
	Attitude	Behavior	Hypnosis	Character
Emotional Disorders ...	196	262	231	221
Migraine and tension headaches	129	190	153	178
Asthma	23	25	25	27
Eczema and allergy	20	31	26	33
Peptic ulcers	17	29	34	30
Assorted psychosomatic conditions	77.5	104.5	91.5	96.5
	462.5	641.5	560.5	585.5

These results indicate quite clearly that attitude modification (462.5) leads the field in order of importance, followed by hypnosis (560.5), character of relationship (585.5) with behavior modification trailing (641.5).

If we wish to test this statistically by the Chi squared test, we would have to conclude that the patients expressed statistically significant preference towards certain treatments. This can be checked by using the multi-sample Kruskall-Wallis test and this gives the same answer (see Appendix D.)

If we take the same question (5) and evaluate it from a different standpoint, we find that the order of importance, as chosen by the patients, is constant, but the difference in values is even more obvious.

Place the numbers of patients who chose each of the four factors as their first choice underneath each other. Do the same for the second, third and fourth choices. Five patients rated all factors of equal importance and eleven patients failed to comment on this question, leaving 220 patients who made a definite choice.

	1st Choice	2nd Choice	3rd Choice	4th Choice	
Attitude Modification	80	69	52	19 =	220
Behavior Modification	32	48	58	82 =	220
Hypnosis	59	55	46	60 =	220
Character of the relationship	49	48	64	59 =	220
	220	220	220	220	

Thus we obtain a table which shows that if we compare the ratio of the first and fourth choices, Attitude Modification scored 421%, Hypnosis scored 98%, and The Character of the Relationship scored 83%, whereas Behavior Modification scored only 39%.

If we subject the above 4x4 contingency table to the Null Hypothesis and Chi squared tests we have to reject the Null Hypothesis that the choice of ranks was independent of actual treatments and conclude that the patients ranked the treatments according to some significant preferences.

If we compare Attitude Modification to each of the other three components of therapy, by the sign test, it shows to a level of significance $\alpha = 0.05$ that the patients chose Attitude Modification as the most important factor and we can be ninety-five percent confident that this is significant.

Therefore, by all the methods used in evaluating the results of question five, Attitude Modification clearly leads as the most important single factor in therapy.

17
Summary
and
Conclusions

When I started to write the summary and conclusions to this book I intended to show, by reasoned statements, that I had indeed proved what I set out to prove. I tried to show that you cannot separate physical illness from mental illness, emotional disorder or behavior disorder; that the concepts of the conscious and unconscious are not opposed to those of conditioning, and that between these two extreme poles can be fitted the theories and practices of Transactional Analysis, Gestalt and Reality Therapy, Assertiveness and Hypnosis.

When the results of my questionnaire began to come in I realized that perhaps the best way of summarizing my findings was to give the figures shown in the answers — I was going to let the patients speak for me.

The results of the questionnaire more than fulfilled my expectations. The massive response (84.4%) indicated that the patients considered this sufficiently important to respond.

The results which surprised me most were that the overall majority (56.4%) had found, after a period of 14.3 months since the end of therapy, they were continuing to grow and mature and become more in command of their lives. This seemed to me to be worth considerably more than the simple loss of symptoms.

The results which did not really surprise me, but confirmed a growing belief, were that of the factors of Attitude Modification, Behavior Modification, Hypnosis and The Character of the Relationship, Attitude Modification was clearly in the lead in order of importance. Although the other three factors were all important, none was as important as modification of attitude, and there is no "school" of therapy of Attitude Modification, and perhaps this is what we need. It appeared that it was not the alteration of overt behavior which initiated change in the patient, as much as alteration of attitudes towards themselves, people and situations.

From the remarks of the patients, at the completion of therapy, it sometimes seemed that a large percentage felt the hypnosis was more important or the character of the relationship had played a greater part. However, with the passage of months or years, as the relationship dimmed and the hypnosis was used (and needed) less frequently, it was their new, more positive, more assertive, more self-respectful attitudes which sustained them through difficult situations and prevented a relapse into the old patterns of anxiety, depression or physical illness.

The attitude and behavior modifications are all covered in this book and hypnosis is explained as thoroughly as possible. I also hope that I have infused some of the character of the relationship which I establish with my patients into the mode and style of presentation.

The last question — patient's comments regarding therapy, which was added as an afterthought, is revealing and I feel bound to give a number of exerpts from the answers to this question because they are real statements from real patients, and they indicate that considerable thought, time and effort were expended in their remarks, for example,

Patient No. 122: "I feel that all the factors in question five are important and cannot be listed in order of importance. Therapy would not be as effective if any one were left out."

Patient No. 47: (Migraine, eight years) "I am more than pleased with the progress I made and even more pleased to let you know that I have not had a headache of a serious nature since starting treatment."

Patient No. 15: (Whiplash injury) "I came for therapy for a whiplash injury of six months' standing. I also lost the menstrual pains of nine years and did not realize how tense I had been."

Patient No. 40: "Before therapy I had migraine about four times a month. Since my therapy 15 months ago, I have only had four headaches, three of which I was able to control myself. I only wish I had known about this type of therapy twelve years ago when the headaches first started."

Patient 139: (Eczema since childhood) "My eczema has never returned since I received treatment from you five years ago."

Patient No. 146: (Hair pulling, patient bald when first seen) "It is wonderful. My hair is now down to my shoulders and I have had it cut since I last saw you."

Patient No. 154 (Severe asthma requiring Prednisone*) "The therapy has helped enormously and I now only occasionally take medication."

Patient No. 43: (Fear of flying) "I have since taken several flights and was pleased that I could do the journey at ease. Before therapy, I had to be tranquillized to get on the plane."

I feel the results of the questionnaire show the method works and that it is more rapid compared with most forms of psychotherapy. It shows the results are far more sustained than those obtained by medications and the combination of methods and techniques used by Analysts, Behaviorists, Gestaltists, Rogerians and the others mentioned produces not only the relief of symptoms but also a growth experience which influences all aspects of our lives.

The different "schools" all have valid portions but they must be joined together into a unified concept and method of therapy and I have tried to show that they can indeed be so drawn together.

I feel that the philosophy of gratitude of Hans Selye is expressing in different terms the same conditions for building Self-Esteem as described by Stanley Coopersmith, and that these conditions are also those which satisfy the needs of the Child in Transactional Analysis.

When you examine them closely you will find that the healthy life position of "I'm O.K. — You're O.K." as described by Tom Harris, is identical with the four conditions required for Becoming a Person, as described by Carl Rogers, and if you study these four conditions of Rogers, it tells you a lot more about how you are to feel "O.K.".

*Prednisone is a powerful medication only used in the most severe forms of asthma.

Many theories, many authors, different styles, different words, complementary and contrasting techniques — all can be woven into a unified concept to deal with the infinitely complex psychosomatic and emotional disorders of man.

I have tried to show that psychological causes are the main factors in precipitating many forms of disorder, and that psychological treatments are the logical, and in many cases, the only treatments which are likely to be permanently effective.

I do not, however, wish to give the impression that all disease is emotional in origin and that the only treatments are psychological. The "Psychosomaticist" must look for organic disease and treat it accordingly.

To illustrate this I would like to present the case of a 45-year-old male who was referred for severe depression, loss of motivation and impotence. He was divorced and had lost custody of his children, which was a bitter blow to him. He had remarried, but had begun to withdraw into himself and would sit in the basement staring at the wall. He had lost all sex drive. His work was deteriorating and he said he was "literally going to pieces".

While I was giving him a physical examination, he said that he often woke in the night feeling terribly cold and had to get more blankets. The physical examination was unremarkable, but I sent a sample of blood for estimation of thyroid function. The result showed that he was suffering from a severely underactive thyroid.

I prescribed a preparation of thyroid hormone and he made a rapid and complete recovery without the aid of psychotherapy. I, therefore, feel that the Psychosomaticist should be, first of all, medically qualified, but orientated and trained to deal with emotionally-induced illness.

To those readers who have gone to their doctor with symptoms and been told, after thorough physical examination and exhaustive investigation, that there is "absolutely nothing wrong with you", I hope this book has not only given you food for thought but also the means of dealing with those symptoms so that there is, in fact, absolutely nothing wrong with you.

I hope that you have found, in this book, something to enable you to change your attitudes and behavior so that you can cope with the Monster in you. May you continue to do so.

I present my views on paper because I have found, from clinical experience, that they have worked for me in dealing with my patients, my family and myself. I hope they may be of help to some of you to enable you to advance further in the process of Becoming; in the never-ending task of Self-Actualization; and to the beginnings of purpose, direction, peace of mind and, hopefully, Health, Happiness and Success.

Appendix A
Case
Histories

I wish to present some short case histories, all of which were treated in the manner explained in chapter fifteen. The object of presenting these cases is to indicate something of the range of conditions which can be successfully treated by this method.

Case No. 1

A 42-year-old lady with one-sided migraine headaches which she has had for many years. She is married and has three children. Her marriage was described as "acceptable", but her husband has never been ill and he considers that she takes too many pills. She keeps her feelings to herself and "bottles them up". I spent the first session with her explaining hypnosis. The next week she came back and hypnosis was induced and she was able to develop a numb hand. She was also able to transfer the numbness to that part of her head where she had her headaches. In this and subsequent sessions we discussed the principles of transactional analysis, the conditions necessary for the establishment of a good self-esteem, her relationship with her husband and other people. I also started her on exercises in assertiveness to enable her to express her feelings effectively but without aggression. I saw her for seven sessions. She had no further headaches after the third session. Her ability to cope with her life situation and her marriage had improved enormously. One year later she reports still having no migraine headaches. She will occasionally get a mild form of tension headache but this she can take away with her self-hypnosis.

Case No. 2

A 31-year-old lady who presented with massive hives all over her body. She had emigrated from England some two and a half years before. She had previously had attacks of hives in England but had not had any since emigrating to Canada. I found, in taking the history, that her sister, whom she had not seen for two and a half years, was staying with her in Canada, and she had always had considerable conflicts with her sister. I explained to her the mechanisms of stress and how she could learn to control this by hypnosis and changes in her attitude and behavior towards her sister. She was seen for a total of seven sessions, at the end of which time she felt much improved. She was not having any attacks of hives. She could cope not only with her sister but also with boyfriends and associates at work. She was expressing her feelings more adequately and felt very pleased with herself.

Case No. 3

A 41-year-old lady who had suffered from asthma from the age of nineteen, but which had become very severe during the last three years. It had increased in severity during the period in which her marriage had been deteriorating, and she had just recently become divorced. She was a school teacher and was having difficulty in teaching because of her constant wheezing. I explained the mechanism of stress, taught her to induce hypnosis, and we began to examine her attitudes and behavior. After two sessions she found her asthma was reduced in incidence from about one attack a day to one minor one a week; she had taken up swimming again and could swim lengths of the pool, whereas previously she had only been able to manage widths. By the sixth session she was almost completely free of wheezing and this only occurred if she put herself under severe stress. Six months later she reports being completely free of asthma, being able to cope with her life situation and feeling very much happier.

Case No. 4

A 46-year-old male with a history of hypertension for thirty years. When I first saw him he was taking over twenty tablets a day. He had been seeing doctors in many areas and all of them had taken his blood pressure and added to his medications. When I took a history from him, I found that his mother had always insisted upon him being about twenty minutes early for school every morning and he had married a wife who was always five minutes late for everything! I found that he was working in a garage as a mechanic and that the mechanic on one side of him was always borrowing his tools and not giving them back, and the mechanic on the other side was always running the engines of cars without connecting up the exhaust hose. He also related how his wife's parents were extremely religious and were trying to ram their religious beliefs down his children's throats. This upset him very greatly but he never expressed his feelings on this or any of the other related matters. First of all I taught him hypnosis, and then we really had to work on his attitude towards his wife's lateness, whether or not it really mattered. We had to role play situations in which he expressed his feelings assertively to the mechanics at work and to his in-laws. I saw him for twelve consecutive weeks at which time his blood pressure was normal and he was completely off medications. I have followed him now for four years and I see him to check his blood pressure about every three months. His blood pressure has remained normal, he is still off pills and he is coping very adequately with life.

Case No. 5

A 23-year-old male with eczema, particularly bad on the arms and legs, which he had had since infancy. It was made worse by stress. He was seen a total of six times, during which his eczema disappeared completely. Even his mother would not believe it because she said the eczema had started when he was a very small baby and she could not believe that this was stress-related. However, eight months later he is still completely clear of his eczema and taking no medications.

Case No. 6

This 28-year-old lady had been suffering from post partum depression following the delivery of her second child some three months previously. She had been hospitalized from the second week after the delivery of the baby for the remainder of the three months and she had been having heavy medication but was not improving. Her parents, who were friends of ours, rang me and asked what they should do. We agreed that she and her husband should come to Calgary and stay with us for a few days. In joint sessions with her husband over a period of only five days we went through the principles outlined in this book, at the end of which time she was feeling much improved. She was totally off medications. Her ability to cope with her life had improved, as had her relationship with her husband. One year later she is still extremely well. This case, I feel, really shows how much more effective and brief the type of therapy outlined in this book can be compared with the more traditional forms of therapy.

Case No. 7

This was a 12-year-old girl who, when I first saw her, was almost completely bald because she was always pulling out her hair. Her mother admitted to having been very hard on her as a child and she had never expressed her feelings well. She had a very poor opinion of herself. Even at this young age, she was able to understand the principles outlined in this book. She learned to relax very quickly and she was given direct suggestions for the strengthening of her self-esteem. She stopped pulling out her hair from the very first session. She was seen seven times over a period of two months, and at that time she was much happier, more outgoing, and her hair was beginning to grow again. One year later she had a beautiful head of hair and was coping with her life, both at home and at school, in a much more effective way.

Case No. 8

A 41-year-old lady presented with an acute anxiety neurosis which had been precipitated by a car accident some six months before in which she had sustained a broken leg. Following the accident she had become extremely nervous and could not stay at home alone. When she went out she would find that she had uncontrollable fits of shaking and would occasionally faint. She was afraid of being in crowds and if she were at a party she had to sit near the door, so that she could get out quickly if she felt an attack of panic coming on. She was seen nine times over a two month period, during which she lost all her symptoms and her tranquillizers were completely stopped. Six months later she reports being one hundred percent better.

Case No. 9

A 32-year-old lady who had severe eczema of her hands. She was, at this time, four months pregnant. She gave a history of having had a very bad delivery with her first baby and was extremely nervous about this pregnancy. She was an extremely good subject and learned to relax very well. Her eczema began to clear from the second session and by the time she had been seen seven times, was gone completely. She subsequently had her baby without any difficulties and she reported that she had hardly felt any discomfort at all during the delivery. One year later she is still well with no evidence of eczema.

Case No. 10

This 35-year-old male was referred for impotence. He had been separated from his wife for two years. He had been living "common-law" with a lady whom he loved very much but was having difficulty in performing the sex act. He had been brought up in a very religious background. His sexual performance had been perfectly normal with his wife, but with his girl friend it was "lousy". We first discussed his attitudes towards his Parent tapes with regard to sin and all the other "mustn't's" and "don't's". He was an extremely good hypnotic subject. He was seen a total of six times. I would like to quote his own description of the improvement in his sexual performance at the end of his visits. He said, "Whereas, at the beginning, it was from damn poor to reasonably good, it is now from very good to fantastic". His feelings of self-esteem had improved enormously, and he also made the interesting observation that his own sense of well being appeared to be rubbing off on his girl friend and she was feeling much happier also.

Case No. 11

A 30-year-old lady with a history of migraine which had started after she had been married for the first time for two years. This first marriage broke up after four years because the husband was a severe alcoholic. She had remarried, two years prior to the onset of treatment, and was having some difficulty with her new in-laws. She worked in a fairly responsible position and had a lot of pressure at work. She was extremely non-assertive and allowed people to walk all over her. She was seen a total of six times, during which she lost her headaches and reported that her sessions had made a great difference to her life. She no longer dreaded waking up in the morning, she was able to cope with her work and was no longer allowing people to push her around. She was enjoying her social life much more and was healthier and happier in every respect.

Appendix B
A Useful
Diagnostic Sign

During the years in which I have been studying the psychosomatic aspects of medicine, I have repeatedly noticed that certain patients have a habit of fluttering their eyelids very rapidly at the exact moment when they are describing their physical symptoms.

At first it was a chance observation that, when this occurred, the symptoms of which the patients was complaining, could not be supported by a physical sign of illness. I noticed this more and more frequently, and also observed that, in severe cases, not only would the eyelids flutter rapidly, but also the eyeballs would turn up momentarily, revealing the whites of the eyes under the iris.

I began to note this on the history sheets as "positive eyelid sign"; and this seemed to correlate exactly with physical symptoms inspired by neurosis. Gradually, over a period of several years, the nurses at the hospital would note "Positive Gorman's Sign".

I have come to the conclusion that the absence of the eyelid sign does not, by any means, exclude the possibility of neurotic symptoms; but that the presence of the sign does, invariably, indicate a high degree of anxiety associated with physical symptoms and either non-existent or unrelated physical signs.

Appendix C
Questionnaire

Patient No. ....

Presenting Symptoms ....

Other Symptoms ....

Length of History ....

Period seen from .... to .... No. times seen .....

Were you on regular medication before treatment? Yes ..... No .....
If so, what? ....

....

(1) How were you at end of treatment? Check most appropriate
    answer.
    (1) Worse
    (2) No change
    (3) Slightly improved
    (4) Very improved
    (5) Complete loss of symptoms
(2) Had your attitude towards yourself changed during treatment?
    (1) Worse
    (2) No change
    (3) Slightly improved
    (4) Very improved
(3) Had your attitude to coping with life situations changed?
    (1) Worse
    (2) No change
    (3) Slightly improved
    (4) Very improved
    (5) Now able to cope with anything

(4) How are you now?

    (1) Worse

    (2) No change

    (3) Maintaining the improvement

    (4) Continuing to improve in your ability to cope

Are you now on regular medication? Yes ..... No ..... If so, what? .

....

(5) What, in your opinion, were the factors most important in therapy? List 1-4 in order of importance.

    ( ) Attitude Modification. Did therapy help you to change your attitudes towards your life, symptoms, situations?

    ( ) Behavior Modification. Did therapy help you to be more effective in dealing with situations?

    ( ) Hypnosis. Was this of considerable help in enabling you to reduce your symptoms?

    ( ) The Character of the Relationship. Do you feel that the type of relationship between us had any bearing on the results of therapy?

Patient's comments regarding therapy.

Appendix D
Statistical
Analysis
of Results

Statistical Analysis of Preferences of Therapy Treatments for Psychosomatic Disorders

The total of 225 patients answered the question ranking the preferences among four treatments: attitude modification, behavior modification, hypnosis, and character. Assuming the null hypothesis H_0 that their responses were at random and did not indicate any statistically significant preferences, the expected rank for each treatment would be 225 x $(1+2+3+4)/4 = 562.5$. This consideration yields the following contingency table:

	Attitude	Behavior	Hypnosis	Character
Observed ranks	462.5	641.5	560.5	585.5
Expected ranks under H_0	562.5	562.5	562.5	562.5

Corresponding X^2-test of goodness of fit yields $X^2 = 29.82$
Corresponding critical value of X^2 with 3 degrees of freedom for $\alpha = .05$ is

$$X^2_{3,.05} = 7.81$$

Hence, we have to reject the null hypothesis that there were no preferences towards different treatments and conclude that the patients expressed statistically significant preferences towards certain treatments.

The same hypothesis can be tested perhaps more appropriately using an alternative multisample Kruskall-Wallis test. In this case

$$H = \frac{N-1}{N} \sum_{i=1}^{K} n_i \; (\bar{x}_i - \tfrac{1}{2} \, (n+1))^2 / \frac{1}{12} \, (n^2-1)$$

$N = 900$ total number of ranks
$n_1 = n_2 = n_3 = n_4 = 225$ number of answers (patients)
$\bar{x}_1 = 2.06$ average rank for attitude modification
$\bar{x}_2 = 2.85$ average rank for behavior modification
$\bar{x}_3 = 2.49$ average rank for hypnosis
$\bar{x}_4 = 2.60$ average rank for character
$n = 4$ maximum rank
$H = 58.65$

The corresponding critical value $X^2_{3,.05} = 7.81$ is the same as before and hence we have to reject again the null hypothesis and make the same conclusion.

We can test also the null hypothesis H_0 that the choice of ranks for treatments is independent of the actual treatments. Thus using X^2-test for the following 4 x 4 contingency table we get

	First Choice	Second Choice	Third Choice	Fourth Choice	
Attitude modification	80	69	52	19	220
Behavior modification	32	48	58	82	220
Hypnosis	59	55	46	60	220
Character of the relationship	49	48	64	69	220
	220	220	220	220	

$X^2 = 71.38$

Corresponding critical value of X^2 with 9 degrees of freedom for $\alpha = .05$ is $X^2_{9,.05} = 16.9$

Hence we have to reject the null hypothesis that the choice of ranks was independent of actual treatments and conclude that patients ranked the treatments according to some significant preferences. All X^2-tests involve dependent data, however, sample size is so large and the data appears to be so highly significant that the tests are properly justified.

In order to determine which pairs of treatments show significant difference in preferences of patients, let us compare attitude modification to other treatments. Let us denote a patient assigning a lower rank to attitude modification by the sign + and let us denote all other patients by the sign –. We would like to test the hypothesis that the patients really preferred the attitude modification treatment. Let

$$p = \text{Probability } (+)$$

Then our null and alternative hypotheses are:

$$H_o: p = \frac{1}{2}$$
$$H_A: p > \frac{1}{2}$$

and we can use the sign test.

Out of $n = 220$ patients who expressed their preferences $x = 157$ preferred the attitude modification to behavior modification treatment.

The corresponding normal score

$$z = \frac{x - np}{\sqrt{npq}} = 6.33$$

The critical value of the normal distribution for $\alpha = .05$ is

$$z_{.05} = 1.645$$

Because $z > z_{.05}$ we have to reject H_0 in favor of H_A.

Similarly for the comparison of attitude modification and hypnosis we have $x = 131$ patients who preferred the former treatment and hence $z = 2.83$. Finally 139 patients preferred attitude modification to the character of relationship and hence $z = 3.91$. In all these cases we have to reject the null hypothesis of indifference.

Hence we have to conclude that the data represent statistically highly significant evidence against indifference among patients towards the treatments and we have to conclude that the patients actually significantly preferred the attitude modification compared to all other treatments. It can be readily seen that we have to accept this claim at any practical level of significance. It is obvious that similarly calculated Wilcoxon matched pairs rank sum test yields the same conclusion.

References

APPENDIX E

Bibliography

1. Berne, Eric. *Transactional Analysis in Psychotherapy.* New York: Graves Press, 1961.
   What Do You Say After You Say Hello. New York: Graves Press, 1970.
   Games People Play. New York: Graves Press, 1964.
   Sex in Human Loving. New York: Pocket Books, 1971.
2. Browne, Harry. *How I Found Freedom in an Unfree World.* New York: MacMillan Publishing, 1973.
3. Coopersmith, Stanley. *The Antecedents of Self-Esteem.* San Francisco: W. H. Freeman, 1967.
4. Cue, Emil. *How to Use Autosuggestion Effectively.* Hollywood: J. H. Duckworth, Wilshire Book, 1960.
5. Erickson, Milton H. *Advanced Techniques of Hypnosis and Therapy.* Selected Papers Edited by Jay Haley. New York and London: Stratton Publishers, 1967.
   Erickson, M., Hershman, S. and Secter, I. *The Practical Application of Medical and Dental Hypnosis.* New York: The Julian Press, 1961.
6. Freud, Sigmund. *A General Introduction to Psycho-Analysis.* New York: Pocket Books, 1952.
   The Interpretation of Dreams. New York: Discus Books, 1965.
   Beyond the Pleasure Principle. New York: Bantam Books, 1928.
   Group Psychology and the Analysis of the Ego. New York: Bantam Books, 1960.

7. Glasser, William. *Reality Therapy.* New York: Harper and Row, 1965.
The Identity Society. New York: Harper and Row, 1972.
Mental Health or Mental Illness? New York: Harper and Row, 1960.

8. Gorman, Brian J. "An Abstract Technique of Ego Strengthening," *American Journal of Clinical Hypnosis,* January, 1974.
"Adjunctive Management of a Grossly Unstable Diabetic by Hypnosis," *Canadian Medical Association Journal,* March, 1974.

9. Hall, Calvin J. *A Primer of Freudian Psychology.* A Mentor Book, New York: The World Publishing Company, 1954.

10. Harris, Thomas A. *I'm O.K. — You're O.K.* New York: Harper and Row, 1967.

11. Hartland, John. *Medical and Dental Hypnosis and Its Clinical Applications.* London: Bailliere, Tundall and Cassell, 1966.
"Further Observations on the Use of Ego-Strengthening Techniques," *American Journal of Clinical Hypnosis,* 1971.

12. James, Muriel and Jongeward, Dorothy. *Born To Win.* Reading, Mass.: Addison-Wesley, 1971.

13. Jourard, Sidney M. *The Transparent Self.* New York: D. Van Nostrand Reinhold, 1971.
Self Disclosure. New York: John Wiley and Sons, 1971.
Disclosing Man to Himself. New York: D. Van Nostrand Reinhold, 1968.

14. Lazarus, Arnold A. *Behavior Therapy and Beyond.* New York: McGraw-Hill, 1971.
Clinical Behavior Therapy. New York: Brunner/Mazel, 1972.

15. Lecron, Leslie M. and Bordeaux, Jean. *Hypnotism Today.* Hollywood: Wilshire Book, 1969.

16. Maslow, Abraham. *Towards a Psychology of Being.* New York: Van Nostrand Reinhold, 1968.
The Farther Reaches of Human Nature. New York: Viking Press, 1971.

17. Maltz, Maxwell. *Psycho-Cybernetics.* Englewood Cliffs: Wilshire Book, 1960.

18. Peale, Norman V. *The Power of Positive Thinking.* New York: Fawcett Publications, 1952.

19. Penfield, Wilder. *The Mystery of the Mind*. Princeton: Princeton University Press, 1975.
    Memory Mechanisms. A.M.A. Archives of Neurology and Psychiatry 67, 1952.

20. Perls, Frederick S. *Gestalt Therapy Verbatim*. Toronto: Bantam Books, 1969.
    Ego Hunger and Aggression. New York: Random House, 1969.

21. Rogers, Carl E. *On Becoming a Person*. Boston: Houghton Mifflin, 1961.
    Carl Rogers on Encounter Groups. New York: Harper and Row, 1970.
    Counselling and Psychotherapy. Cambridge, Mass.: Houghton Mifflin, 1942.
    Rogers, Carl and Dymond, Rosalind. *Psychotherapy and Personality Change*. Chicago: University of Chicago Press, 1954.

22. Salter, Andrew. *Conditioned Reflex Therapy*. New York: Capricorn Books, 1949.
    The Case Against Psychoanalysis. New York: Citadel Press, 1968.
    What is Hypnosis. New York: Citadel Press, 1944.

23. Selye, Hans. *The Stress of Life*. New York: McGraw-Hill, 1956.
    Stress Without Distress. Toronto: McClelland and Stewart, 1974.
    "Stress," *The Rotarian*, March, 1978.

24. Skinner, B. F. *About Behaviorism*. New York: Alfred A. Knopf, 1974.

25. Smith, Manuel J. *When I Say "No" I Feel Guilty*. New York: Bantam Publishing, 1975.

26. Steiner, Claude. *Games Alcoholics Play*. New York: Ballantine Books, 1971.

27. Szasz, Thomas S. *The Myth of Mental Illness*. New York: Dell Publishing, 1961.

28. Truax, C. B. and Carkhuff, R. T. *Towards Effective Counselling and Psychotherapy*. Chicago: Aldine Publishing, 1967.

29. Watson, John B. *Behaviorism*. New York: W. W. Norton, 1924.

30. White, Robert W. "A Preface to the Theory of Hypnosis," *Journal of Abnormal Soc. Psychology*, October, 1941.

Index